I0425072

In Loving Memory
Of My Daughter,
DeAnne

The Consequences of Alcohol

May 1975. With sweating palms, a racing heart, and cotton-mouth, I sat down close to my mother who was finishing up another project on her sewing machine. Finally my lips parted and the words came out, "Mom, I went to the doctor and found out I am pregnant."

Pausing briefly, but without missing a stitch, she said casually, "I'm not surprised." Being brought up in a strict Catholic family, that wasn't the response I had expected. But since I was far from an angel, her reaction wasn't all that much of a surprise either. We talked calmly about what my plans were for my baby and her father. There was no question in my mind. Since her father wanted nothing to do with me after I told him I was pregnant, he was not going to be a part of our lives. However from the moment the nurse confirmed my pregnancy there was no doubt in my mind I would have and keep my baby. From an early age, at a Catholic school, I learned about making babies. Even though I didn't have a clear understanding of what that meant, I did understand what the feeling was in my heart and that was the desire to have a baby, someone I could share an unconditional love with for the rest of my life.

A few months earlier I had turned eighteen and dropped out of high school. Mom and Dad eventually came to accept my situation, but before the baby was born I moved out and shuffled from one lousy living situation to another. In my fifth month I met a man that seemed very shy and willing to accept both my baby and me as his own. We married three months after we met, which certainly was not long enough for me to know what I had gotten myself into. Because I was pregnant and this man truly seemed to want to take care of me, we married ten weeks before the baby was to arrive. Since my parents were devout Catholics, I felt like the least I could do for them was get married, otherwise I was going to be an unwed mother as well as a high school dropout. By marrying this stranger I thought I was doing something right. Since my heart had ached for so long to have a child I thought I could handle all of the complications that I would be facing because my baby would give me the strength. Besides, suddenly it seemed that I had a purpose. There was going to be someone in this world who would love me, want me and need me no matter what. Nothing would ever compare to the elation I felt when leaving the doctor's office, except December 27, 1975, the day my daughter, DeAnne, was born.

Saturday, September 8, 2001. They stumbled down the stairs of the quaint, rustic burger-n-beer joint, their voices loud and sounding a little argumentative. Their entrance and their looks attracted the attention of the other patrons, most of whom were the up-scale yuppies that often visited such social clubs while in Glenwood Springs, Colorado. There were also a few who, like DeAnne and Keith, appeared to be hippies born in the wrong era. Both in their 20's, they were dressed in tie-dyed T-Shirts and Doc Marten sandals. They both had long blonde hair that was tied back in ponytails and the tops of their heads were covered with bandanas. They sat at the bar and ordered two or three drinks each before they decided to leave around 11:15 p.m. that Saturday night. The air was cool but neither of them really noticed, with the amount of alcohol they had in their systems, and the heavy wool sweaters they had thrown over their heads as they hopped on the red Kawasaki Ninja bullet bike. Keith tore away from the curb and headed to the nearest convenience store where DeAnne ran in and picked up some Hamburger Helper and a package of ground turkey. They sped away from the store and onto the highway in hopes of getting home early enough to hook up with their friend Mark at the apartment he shared with DeAnne.

Mark on the other hand was waiting impatiently. Even though he was convinced that DeAnne's relationship with Keith was purely platonic he still didn't like the fact that they were spending so much time together, especially since Mark was semi-confined to the area workhouse due to alcohol-related offenses. That night he was released on a pass but had to turn himself back into custody by midnight and was hoping to spend some time alone with his girlfriend before doing that. By 11:15 p.m. he had to give up waiting and hopped on the next city bus going back to jail. In his cell, he couldn't sleep wondering where DeAnne was.

Sunday, September 9, 2001. The temperature was around 70 degrees by 10:30 a.m., and the sun was shining. It was an unusually nice day for that time of year in Minnesota. We were planning our usual Sunday morning walk and breakfast, when we noticed two uniformed officers coming to the front door. Since I had tested positive for marijuana use in a job application process the Friday before I thought for some reason that's why they were there. Why else would the Carver County Sheriffs be at the door? One of the officers began pounding with determination, so nervously I went to the kitchen window and asked if there was something I could help them with. They asked if my name was MaryLee. I responded with a confused and frightened "Yes." They asked me to come to the door but I was afraid they might be there to arrest me so I told them it wasn't a good time and asked if they could come back later–ridiculously thinking they would actually do that if they were there to arrest me! Needless to say they continued to pound on the door as I tried desperately to come up with another excuse why not to answer it. Finally, I asked again why they were there. After another long pause one the officers asked if I had a daughter named DeAnne.

Since she had been in her share of trouble during her adolescent years, and at that particular time had a warrant out for her arrest, I wasn't really surprised (and somewhat relieved) that they were asking about her. "Did she get into some kind of trouble?" I asked. The officer insisted that I open the door. "Can't you just tell me?" I pleaded again. Four seconds later, my life changed forever. Four seconds was how long it took for the officer to say the words, "Ma'am, I regret to inform you that your daughter was killed in a motorcycle accident last night."

After a couple of years of dating, James and Lorraine were married in the fall of 1950. It was a fairly large wedding since Lorraine came from a family of seven children. It took place in her hometown of Hartington, Nebraska. She was a beautiful bride, wearing a cream colored satin gown with a long, lacey train draping down her back. Her long black hair fell freely from under her delicate veil. James was very slender and handsome. He also had thick, wavy, black hair. His mother was the only one to attend the ceremony from his side of the family. His father had died several years before, and his two sisters could not afford the long trip from northern Minnesota to Nebraska.

Soon after they were married, they moved to Minneapolis where James found a job as a machinist with a major industrial company. Lorraine continued her education at a girl's school in the city. In October, a year after they were married, their first daughter was born. She had curly, auburn hair that framed her round face. Her round nose gave her the "she looks just like her father" appearance. A year later Lorraine became pregnant again, so in July 1953, Julia was born. Little Cheryl instinctively took the role of caretaker. Since they had just moved into their new home a week before, her mommy needed all the help she could get. Cheryl did a good job of taking care of herself whenever she could, and letting her mommy know when the new baby was crying. Around the same time that Cheryl was potty trained and Julia was walking, Jackie was born. Her hair was the same deep brown, almost black that Julia's was except Jackie's didn't seem to have as much curl as her older sisters' did. As soon as she had her first taste of formula it became apparent that her tummy just couldn't handle it, and she seemed to have some difficulty breathing, which would be diagnosed as asthma.

Toward the end of July, 1956, Lorraine was told that her fourth child was on the way. The doctor said she could expect this one around the end of February or the first of March.

On March 1, 1957, she was rudely awakened by the first gripping contraction. She turned to notice that it was 2 a.m. and her "Ole" was not in bed beside her. For an instant she panicked at the thought of how she would get to the hospital without him. Then she heard him in the kitchen and called out to him. When he came into the bedroom, he found her taking deep breaths. He knew right away that it was time, since he had been through the same signs with her in labor three times before. They notified the doctor and woke her mother to let her know that she was in charge of the other girls. Grandma Millie was familiar with the routine too, since she had come up from Nebraska to help with each new baby.

James and Lorraine put their coats and boots on as they talked about how lucky they were that March had come in like a lamb. It was still pretty cold, but at least they didn't have to deal with one of the blizzards of the past. It was fortunate that they left when they did, however, because the doctor hadn't even arrived when I did. I just couldn't wait. So at 4:20 a.m., MaryLee arrived kicking and screaming and struggling to survive, unaware that most of her life would be spent kicking and screaming and struggling to survive.

(2)

Being born with the same dark, curly hair that my older sisters had, I looked just like they did at birth. But in a short time people started to notice how uniquely blue my eyes were, a shade that would always draw comments. The fact that I was a colicky baby made me difficult at first. After I outgrew that, I was treated as the princess of the family, mostly with the attention and affection that my dad showered on me. One afternoon before I started nursery school, Mom dressed me up, positioning the curls around my face just right. She told me that my daddy was going to take me to work with him. It was so exciting to think that I was going to see where he worked and meet his friends all by myself. Undivided attention was a rare treat.

Dad seemed like a different person as we entered the noisy building. At home he was pretty quiet, but there he was very sociable as if everyone was his friend. He seemed very proud to be showing off one of his pretty babies. But when we returned to the car, the dad I knew reappeared. No more smiling. No more laughing. No more conversation.

Three years later it became obvious that the latest addition to the family, Danielle, was getting some of the attention that I was used to. It was difficult to understand. For three years I had been the star attraction, but suddenly I was just another one of the girls. It was even more difficult to adjust to the lack of attention when the sixth daughter was born, eighteen months after Danielle. Penny was a doll. She had the same dark, curly hair and blue eyes that most of us had. But there was something about Penny that made her a little more special than the rest of us. At least Mom and Dad seemed to think so. Maybe because they knew she would be the last. Along with the arrival of the latest princess in November 1961, there were other things happening in the household that would not only change my position of importance but affect the whole family.

Julia had begun to show signs of asthma, the same illness that had already afflicted Jackie. Her adolescent years were spent just trying to stay alive. Night after night Mom would sit up with her, trying to get her to calm down and get control of her breathing. Month after month she would end up in the intensive care unit. Julia excelled in school mainly because her activities were so limited. The slightest bit of exertion would provoke an attack. So she spent most of her time reading. And we would spend most of the time waiting for another attack.

Dad was spending most of his time coming home from work and ordering one of us to comb his hair or rub his feet until he would fall asleep in his favorite chair. He would wake up for dinner, eat, and return to his original position. More times than not we would wish that he would have slept through dinner because he usually managed to make it a miserable time for all of us. If we spilled our milk or, God forbid, choked, he would tap his fork on the table until we cleaned up the mess, stopped choking, or started crying. It was a rare occasion if one of us didn't end up in tears at the dinner table every night. Sometimes when Mom would come home from her part-time job at a fabric store she would ask how Dad was if he was asleep. I would show her by imitating him bouncing from wall to wall as he was going to the bedroom or to his chair. It was never a good idea to have friends over because we never knew what kind of a mood Dad was going to come home in. But one day I did invite a school friend over knowing that Dad would be at a meeting and when he got home he probably would go right to sleep. I was wrong. He should have gone to bed, but he didn't. Instead he hollered upstairs asking if there was someone up there. When I told him I had a friend visiting he barked at me to call it a day. Foolishly, I asked if she could stay awhile longer, but after being rebuked, and very embarrassed, I escorted my friend to the door. Although I could not understand his reasoning I knew better than to question him. My friend asked me if I was scared. She said when her dad came home "like that" she got scared.

More confused than scared, I told her. But as we stood at the back door I suddenly decided that staying in the house alone with him didn't sound like a very good idea. Even though there was nothing I felt I had done wrong for him to be so angry at me, there was no one else at home for him to take his frustrations out on, so I dashed out the door with my friend and ran to the bus stop where my mother would be arriving soon. As soon as she got off the bus and looked at me she knew something was wrong. I told her Dad was acting weird and blew up at me for no apparent reason. Mom assured me that I did nothing wrong and that she would deal with the situation when she got home or whenever he woke up, preferring the latter. Fortunately, he was passed out and remembered nothing, or at least said nothing about his behavior, in the morning.

Every year families belonging to the Knights of Columbus gathered for their annual picnic. Since both Mom and Dad were members we faithfully attended the dreaded occasions every year, and I hated it. That was unquestionably Dad's favorite time to humiliate me and he did a great job of it. Each summer when I was between the ages of 9 and 12 he would insist that I participate in the children's running races. And every year because I was so overweight and uncoordinated, I would lose, no matter how much or how loud he would scold me for running so slow. It was such a relief when I was too old to participate in the races.

That would not be the only time that those terrible feelings of degradation would appear during my adolescent years. For eight lonely years I attended a Catholic school. Even though I never really had any friends I always seemed to have the ability to make people laugh. Sometimes it was because it was the smelly egg salad sandwiches that Mom would pack in my lunch, or the way I had to wear my hair, bangs cut straight across and way above my eyebrows. But usually it was just because I was fat, nerdy, and fun to laugh at. The only time I was permitted into any cliques was when I was the center of their jokes.

My relationship with my mother was not what could be described as a close one when I was growing up. She was a good mother in that she would make sure that we had clean clothes and food on the table, but saying 'I love you,' or putting her arms around me was foreign nature to her. If I would try to approach her for a hug she would oftentimes stand with her hands at her sides or pat me on the back. Clearly expressing her love in words or actions was nearly impossible for her. Mom always made sure that we participated in church activities. We were expected to attend a Catholic school for eight years and attend Mass at least every Sunday. Sometimes I would dread going to church so much on Sunday morning that I would wake up with a stomach ache that would not go away until it was over. It seemed that every week the smell of stale alcohol would permeate the air. If it wasn't my own dad beside me, it was the old man behind me.

We were also expected to go to confession every week or two. It never really made any sense to me why we had to go through the ritual, except that the consequences for me not going would be burning in hell. Most of the time I would make up sins fearing that if I didn't confess something I was a sinner. The priests, nuns, and my parents drilled it into my head that my successes had nothing to do with me succeeding, but my mistakes meant hellfire.

The feeling of being a misfit was pretty hard to shake. Along with being the brunt of everyone's jokes at school, my sisters would often sarcastically refer to me at the "retard" or "black sheep" of the family. When I was sent to spend week-ends with my uncle and his family and none of my sisters went along, it was a relief, but a curiosity. It was nice to get away from the chaos at home, but sometimes it felt like everyone just wanted to get rid of me. My uncle always had that nasty alcohol smell on his breath that I was all too familiar with, but often his behavior was frightening and upsetting. He too enjoyed making children cry. Whether it was climbing into bed with me after a night of heavy drinking to try to get me to masturbate him (which was unsuccessful since I was only a child) or forcing me to watch him butcher a chicken, he always seemed to think he was funny.

By the time I reached high school, my body, relationships, and behavior changed. Through bicycle riding during most of the summer before, my looks had changed completely by the time I reached junior high school. With tuition getting to be too expensive for my parents we agreed that a public school was the way for me to go. Finally, I was able to get some time away from the church. When I entered the new school people looked at me strangely and giggled, something I was all too familiar with. It was several weeks before I started to realize it was for the opposite reason than at Catholic school. My body had taken on a complete transformation. I had become very slender, except for my unusually large breasts, which made boys and men take notice.

At fourteen years old, it was very difficult to get around. My parents were always too busy to cart me around, which wasn't always a bad thing since they wouldn't have given me a ride anyway had they known where I was going.

Of course there was always the bus, but that cost money, and only nerds took the bus. For my friends and me the most common form of transportation was hitchhiking. Because of my large breasts, tiny butt, and pretty face, getting a ride by posing on the curb with my arm above my head and my thumb out was no problem. The fear of injury, rape, or death never entered my mind. Like most kids my age, we thought we were indestructible, or maybe we just didn't care.

(4)

Since I appeared to be much older than I was, it was always easy for me to meet older people, usually men. During one of my hitchhiking excursions a black male, at least ten years older than me, picked me up and decided that he would be the one to show me exactly how babies were made. It was very painful and scary, but the smell of his incense and the sound of Jimi Hendrix on his stereo, along with his calm and soothing voice, persuaded me to go along with his instructions. For weeks I imagined all kinds of scenarios that would unfold if I was to get pregnant – especially by a black man, since my dad was nothing short of prejudice. Fortunately it was not a worry.

My mother had some of my sisters and I attend Alateen off and on for several years. Sitting around in a circle exchanging bitch stories about our parents got old after awhile, so eventually it was just an excuse for me to meet up with my latest boyfriend. It got to a point where I wouldn't come home for a few days and finally ended up in a juvenile center with a case of gonorrhea. When I returned to the Alateen meetings on a fairly regular basis there was a new boy there. He seemed very bashful, but funny. He talked about how his dad acted after drinking alcohol and how much he hated it. My older sister developed a strong crush on him, but was heart-broken when he called and asked me out on a date. He wasn't exactly my type, but he was nice enough to go out with, so after apologizing to Jackie, we did. Tim and I ended up dating all through high school.

Tim graduated from high school with honors and enrolled in pilot instruction. By that time school didn't matter to me at all. Most days I would usually check in for attendance and leave. Eating up to a hundred hits of white crosses a day made it impossible for me to sit still in a class. Tim introduced me to marijuana, which really didn't affect me the way speed did, pumping me full of energy all the time.

My high school counselor was great for getting me back into school if I had skipped several days in a row. He loved to see me, or maybe look at me is more accurate. He always had to touch me when I was in his office. Sometimes it was just a pat on my hand; other times a slow stroke up my thigh. As long as he wrote the pass I didn't care. While Tim became more interested in his education, my counselor became more interested in me. During one of his visits the familiar smell of stale liquor filled his tiny office. Disregarding the fact that I mentioned it, he pulled my chair closer to him and slid his hand around my hips as he suggested I come over to his house after school for more counseling. He also suggested that I not mention the visit to my parents. He gave me a piece of paper with his address and phone number on it, then wrapped an arm around me, pulling me toward him while his other hand landed suspiciously near the small of my back. He gently kissed the top of my head and held me closer. It felt good even though I knew it was wrong.

That night I showed up at his house and after a brief welcome the counselor offered me a drink of Vodka. I knew I wasn't going to like the taste of it, but I was too nervous to say no. After a few disgusting sips his groping hands were all over me. Suddenly I felt repulsed and had to leave, but not before receiving strict orders not to tell. A few weeks later he highly recommended that I drop out of high school. Considering the fact that I was short several credits and would not be able to graduate with my class anyway, I took his advice and dropped out during the spring of my senior year, right around my eighteenth birthday.

(6)

My first working experience was cashiering at a shoe repair shop in the mall near where I lived. After leaving school I decided to look for something with a little higher pay and prestige, so I applied at an electronics store in the same mall. With a few bats of my big blue eyes and a low cut blouse, I was hired on the spot – much to the relief of everyone at home. Between the mega-doses of white crosses, the break-up with Tim, having an affair with my counselor, leaving school, and underneath the sadness, hurt, and depression I was feeling, I was a nasty person to live with.

One day while I was at work a man from the pet shop next door came over to my store with a little, black, curly-haired puppy. He set it on the counter and wished me a Happy Easter. It broke my heart when he told me that someone had dropped a few of the puppies off and said they couldn't take care of them. He said he needed to find homes for them and he was sure I could take good care of one. When I got home with her my mother was not happy. She stayed for several weeks before it was clear I wasn't home enough to care for her and Mom didn't want to do it anymore, so I surrendered her to an animal shelter.

But with the puppy came the relationship with the donor, Paul, the man from the pet store, who was spending more and more time at my store while I was working. Finally he found the nerve to ask me to join him for dinner some time. His beautiful blue eyes and deep dimples, along with his charm, made me agree to meet him a few nights later. Still reeling from the rejection of Tim and the seduction of the counselor, I fell for all of the magic that Paul seemed to offer. He took me out for dinner at nice places and paid with a credit card. When I asked him why he was signing someone else's name he casually told me it belonged to his boss who had given him permission to use it. He would also rent hotel rooms for us to spend time in.

One evening we stayed at a hotel where we shared a suite with another couple. The room was luxurious dressed in black and red. We shared a few cocktails and moved the furniture around so that each couple would have a little privacy. While we were making out under the sheets I reminded him that I was not on birth control at that time and if we had sex I would most likely become pregnant. Over and over he told me how much he cared about me and how he would take care of me and the baby if that were to happen. I believed him and let him have me. Minutes later when he was finished with me he jumped up from the bed and into the shower.

While he was gone I noticed blood all over the sheets, so when he returned I quickly gathered my clothes and dashed to the bathroom. When I returned from the shower he handed me a twenty dollar bill and said he had already called me a cab to go home. Feeling embarrassed and dirty, I snatched the money from his grasp and sarcastically thanked him. While sitting in the darkness on the cold back seat of the cab, I played the evening over and over in my mind and wondered what I did to deserve being treated like that. Part of me didn't care because I knew I was pregnant.

For the next few days Paul tried to make up for his behavior by picking me up in his boss's limousine, wining and dining me. Because he was ten years older I kept my relationship with him hidden from my parents, knowing there was no way they would approve. So most times he would pick me up and drop me off a few blocks away from the house. As the days turned to weeks I reminded Paul that it was quite possible I was pregnant. He seemed less and less concerned, especially when I confirmed my suspicions.

My period had been late long enough that I decided to take a pregnancy test, so one day after work I walked over to the doctor's office. After telling the receptionist why I was there, she handed me a small cup and directed me to the restroom then back to the waiting area. The waiting felt like an eternity until finally the nurse returned to the waiting area and called my name. It was positive! I was definitely going to have the baby I had wanted for so long! But as expected, Paul only gave me grief when I told him I was in fact pregnant. After denying he could have anything to do with it he had his phone number changed and disappeared. It only stung a little since I wanted the baby for myself anyway.

(7)

By the end of my third month I decided I had to tell my parents. Over and over I rehearsed my speech until I finally had the courage to approach Mom. She had been sitting downstairs in her sewing area working on the doll clothes that she loved to make. The closer I got to her, the faster my heart beat, until I was trembling when I finally reached the bottom of the stairs. It took several minutes for me to open my mouth, but finally the stuttering words came out. I don't know what kind of a reaction I expected, but I didn't expect to hear the calm in her voice when she said she wasn't surprised.

The next night after finishing dinner my sisters were excused from the table but my mother told me to stay seated. After everyone vanished she looked at me in a way that I knew what she expected. The words wouldn't come out so finally Dad spoke up. His eyes bulged as they always did when he was about to explode, then, like the calm before the storm, he told me he already knew. Mom told him earlier. He just wanted to know what my plans were and who the guy was. I told him the same thing I told Mom. The guy was history, the baby wasn't, and that was it. Nothing much was said after that even after my tummy started to swell.

My parents didn't directly say anything about how my situation affected them, but I assumed I had to be an embarrassment to them, so I started looking for other places to live and found a most unhealthy one with an acquaintance who managed a liquor store nearby. He told me he needed someone to take care of his apartment, wash the clothes, keep things tidy, and make an occasional meal in exchange for a sleeping area at no charge. At the time it seemed like a great opportunity so I offered my services and moved in a few days later. But the arrangement came to an abrupt end one evening when Jim came home after a softball game along with the team members he sponsored. He was so drunk he had to use the wall to walk from one room to the other so I went to the bedroom, hoping they would all leave soon.

A few minutes later Jim came in the bedroom and told me he had a proposition for me. Since I was penniless I considered any chance to make a dime but not the one he offered, which was to have sex with all of the members of the softball team for a hundred dollars. That seemed like a lot of money to me at the time, but I asked him what would happen if I said no. He casually chuckled as he told me I had no choice then left the room. Seconds later a strange man staggered into the bedroom and asked why I wasn't undressed yet. Slowly I started to unbutton my jeans hoping he would notice I was pregnant. Even though I was only a few months along, on my 98-pound frame I was beginning to show. But it didn't stop him. I turned my head as he crawled on top of me, noticed the wedding ring on his finger, and wondered what his wife would think about him if she were to see what he was doing to me.

The second man came in and repeated the offense. He too was wearing a wedding band. Finally the third man had the sense to realize that something was very wrong. He handed me my clothes and told me to get dressed and leave, that he would handle Jim. He left the room but returned a few minutes later to let me know they were taking Jim out. He also suggested that I move out as soon as possible.

That night I was talking to a friend on the phone while she was at a party. I told her what just happened and asked if there were any nice guys in attendance where she was. She told me there was one guy there, named Todd, who was kind of weird but seemed like a nice guy. She put him on the phone and after we talked for several minutes he agreed to come and pick me up so we could get to know each other better. During our conversation he mentioned a mutual acquaintance of ours who was looking for a roommate. We quickly moved in together but when the girl realized how much time Todd was going to spend there she almost immediately moved out. By mid-September Todd and I were making plans to get married even though I knew I didn't love him. I just thought it would be better than trying to raise my baby alone. Besides, I thought, maybe if Tim got wind of this he would rescue me from this mistake. But he didn't.

Todd and I married on October 18, 1975 at his parent's insistence before the baby was born. Even though they knew that my baby was not his, they told all of their friends and relatives that it was. They had made up a fantastic story about the wonderful love affair their adoring son had and how he decided to do the proper thing by marrying me before my due date at the end of December. I went along with it. But a week before the wedding I saw a side of Todd that I hadn't seen before. We had argued about where the reception would be, who would have the wedding and baby showers for me and stag party for him, amongst other things when I decided to leave the room and take a shower. Afterwards I went into the bedroom where I sat on the edge of the bed and wrapped my hair up in a towel. He continued ranting and raving about something trivial when I felt a strong blow to the side of my head. It wasn't enough to knock me out, but it definitely startled me. After rewrapping my hair I glared at him and demanded that he never touch me like that again.

Regardless of the laws of Catholicism we married in the Catholic Church I was brought up in. At that time the idea of an eighteen-year-old girl who was seven months pregnant marrying at the altar was completely sacrilegious. (Needless to say finding a maternity wedding dress wasn't easy either, but Mom and I found a casual, cream colored tent dress on a clearance rack for twenty dollars that served the purpose.) The only people in attendance were a few close relatives and friends, by no means the wedding I had fantasized having while growing up.

The ceremony was small and brief. All of the photographs were taken above my waist, at Mom's suggestion. Todd was his usual irritable self. The way he recited his vows was less than sincere, sounding as if he would have preferred to forget the whole thing and go back home with his parents. The reception was no better. When it came time for us to perform the tradition of feeding each other a piece of wedding cake, he scolded me in front of everyone for missing his mouth. Actually, it seemed as if everyone there would have preferred to be somewhere else, but I tried to make the best of the situation. When the champagne was opened I fought the urge to drink a bottle by myself. I knew as long as I was pregnant I wouldn't touch a drop of alcohol for fear it would somehow damage my baby.

Soon after we were married Todd started to display other strange behavior. He refused to work for fear I would have an affair. He refused to do anything without me or let me do anything without him, even if it was a trip to the grocery store or a visit with my parents. Telephone calls that were dialed wrong would cause ridiculous accusations and suspicions. He made me feel imprisoned and constantly fearful of another fit of anger and flying objects.

One afternoon in mid-November there was an unexpected knock at the door of the apartment where Todd and I still lived. As always I peeked out the peephole and saw two men that I didn't recognize. Instantly I was afraid that Todd would suspect something absurd no matter who the men were. When I asked who they were they identified themselves as postal investigators holding a badge up to the little window and asking to see me. Todd sat glaring in the living room as I let the officers in. They asked if I knew Paul. They said they were investigating a stolen credit card ring that Paul was involved in. Todd got up and stormed down the hall to our bedroom, slamming the door behind him.

The officers continued to ask me questions regarding the use of the credit card Paul told me belonged to his boss. Turned out it was stolen and I had naively signed for purchases at one of the hotels. I didn't have a clue the cards were stolen. I went on to explain my relationship with him as I patted my swollen tummy. I told them I didn't know what happened to Paul and I didn't care. The only thing I knew for sure was that I was going to get it once the officers left. Whether Todd would tear out of the parking lot and disappear for a few hours or stick around and once again use me as his target for whatever object was handy, I didn't know. Surprisingly he didn't flip out. He almost seemed to understand the predicament I was in. But I still looked over my shoulder for the rest of the day. The officers never returned.

Near the end of November my doctor said I had begun to dilate and that the baby could come any time. But by the end of December when I still hadn't given birth we decided to induce labor. He scheduled me to come in at 8:00 a.m. December 27th and prepare to become a mother.

As soon as I arrived at the hospital I was led into a small room, where the nurse told me to undress and lie down on the examining table. She left the room and returned a few moments later handing me a small pill and instructing me to place it under my tongue. A half hour or so later when the labor still hadn't begun she gave me another pill. Within minutes the first pain hit.

Around 11 a.m. the pains had become very intense and regular, and I was getting scared. "Where's my mom?" I asked my husband. He was nervous and did not want to leave me but offered to call her. While he was out the nurse gave me my first humiliating experience with an enema. Todd returned a few moments later and assured me that my mother was on her way, mumbling that he hoped she was anyway. It seemed odd for this man who only seemed to know anger to actually show some concern.

By the time Mom arrived the pains had become almost unbearable. And the more intense they became the more frightened and frustrated I became. My only comfort came from Mom when she assured me that everything would be okay, but then she left almost immediately. She insisted she had to go to work, leaving me feeling hurt and upset. It didn't matter that my dad wasn't there, but I really needed my mother.

One of my sisters was studying in the medical field and came to the hospital wanting to witness a live birth. She and I never got along so I knew she wasn't there to comfort me, but in a way she did, just by her presence. But the doctor would only allow one family member in and unfortunately for her, Todd decided to accompany me. In the delivery room I turned into something demon-like, screaming and swearing at the doctor and everyone else in the room. The doctor had to tell the nurses to keep the gas mask on me just to muffle the vulgarities coming out of my mouth. But once I delivered I immediately calmed down and felt a little embarrassed by the verbal assault I'd spewed out on everyone.

(10)

At 2:38 p.m. that Saturday afternoon, December 27, 1975, my precious baby girl was born. As soon as I looked at her I saw Paul. He had very deep dimples in both cheeks and so did she. They were the first physical feature I noticed. She had my eyes, a unique blue-green, with long dark eyelashes. She was so beautiful, so magical that I could not take my eyes off of her, feeling a love that I had never felt before. Finally, the beloved child I had always dreamed about was in my arms. Tears streamed down my cheeks as I watched her take her first breath and heard her first cry.

After the umbilical cord was cut my baby had to be taken from me for her first bath, but the nurse assured me that I would be reunited with her shortly. I couldn't wait to get to my room and hold her again, so when I got there it seemed like an eternity before she was returned. The nurse wheeled the transparent crib into my room. All I could see was a little tiny bundle of blankets, and a pink cap. The nurse reached in and handed me the most beautiful little person I had ever seen. My baby was sound asleep, but gently sucking on her fist, signaling the need for her first feeding. Beaming, I opened my gown, and gently nursed her, quietly weeping with amazement at this incredible gift I'd been given. Remembering an adorable little girl I had cared deeply for during my babysitting years, I vowed to name my first daughter after her and my best friend from high school, so DeAnne became her name.

A few days after she was born DeAnne and I, along with her step-father, returned back to our tiny, dingy apartment. The angry outbursts became more frequent and intense. What I feared the most was that my innocent baby might get caught up in it somehow, so protecting her was always on my mind. It was a relief when Todd would go to work and I could just enjoy the time with DeAnne. Unfortunately, that relief was short-lived when I discovered that he never had a job. He was leaving the house and driving around, he said, but hadn't worked a day for several weeks. When it became clear that he was not going to work, I knew I had to do something, so I applied for a job at a convenience store two blocks away from our apartment. Leaving my baby with someone I did not trust was very difficult, but I tried to make the best of things by running home on my breaks to check on her, feed her, and change her, none of which Todd would normally do. Although he hadn't lost his temper with her yet, I worried constantly.

One afternoon when I came home from work, DeAnne was sleeping in her crib. Shortly after I came in, she began to cry. When I went into her room and checked her diaper I could not believe what I saw. Her tiny little body was covered with bruises. Her butt, her back, her head, her arms were all black and blue. I screamed for Todd, knowing immediately that he was responsible. He came around the corner of her bedroom looking scared and guilty. For a moment I forgot to be afraid of him. I was beyond furious. It wasn't me he hit this time – it was my baby!

The instant he saw my face he tried blubbering some kind of justification for what he had done, saying she wouldn't stop crying. All I could do was scream at him to get out while I backed him out of the apartment, slamming and locking the door behind him. She was only three months old! I snugly wrapped the innocent little baby in a blanket while sobbing and telling her how sorry I was. After an intervention with both of our parents, it was decided that it was my fault for not being home with my baby, therefore there was no need to notify the police, and Todd promised it would never happen again.

When I found out soon after his attack on DeAnne that I was pregnant again, I certainly did not feel the same elation that I did when I found out I was pregnant with my first. Not because I didn't want another child, but because I did not want his child. I wanted to get away from him, but now it seemed that I would be imprisoned by this evil man even longer. The situation became more intense when Todd joined the army and we were forced to move to the state of Virginia, hundreds of miles away from home where I knew no one.

The violent outbursts continued, even after our son was born almost exactly one year after DeAnne. Over and over I would have to put myself between my babies and him even when I was nursing. All I could do was try to block the blows or beg him to hit me instead of them. A few times I would call the M.P.'s on him, but each time they treated me as if it was all my fault and I was just a bother to them, so I quit calling for help.

By late spring, Todd was sent back to Minnesota for a short time before he went on to Oklahoma. I was so relieved to get back home. Silently I promised my children that we would not travel on with him. The day he left my mind was made up that I needed to stay away from him. He called several times a day sometimes crying, sometimes threatening to hurt me somehow, if I did anything to betray him, many times following his threats with a sick and sinister chuckle. He was so obsessed with what I was doing that he was finally given an honorable discharge because of mental instability. When he told me he was returning to Minnesota a few weeks after he left I was sick. Once again I was going to be stuck a little longer since I had no place to go but with him. During the weeks he was gone my parents let me stay with them, but having a six- and eighteen-month-old in the house was tough on them and us.

Within weeks of our finding an apartment together Todd was flipping out on us again. I couldn't take it anymore and decided to ask my mother what she might suggest. Being the devout Catholic that she was the thought of divorce was not an option, even when I told her of the abuse. She did however suggest that I see the priest that married us for some counseling to see if he could help us through our problems. It seemed futile to take that step under the circumstances but I knew I would not get her help or support unless the priest agreed to annul the marriage.

Finally I got permission from both the priest and my mother to file for a divorce, so even though I was scared to death that he would find out, I went to a free legal clinic during a brief moment when I could disappear without questions. Each visit to the lawyer was stressful but gave me such relief at the time. I just wanted to collect my babies and get away from Todd. During the last week of November my attorney and the police were on stand-by while Todd was to be served with divorce papers and a restraining order. However, the day before he was to be served he was broadsided in his car when someone ran a red light, and he was severely injured. As soon as his friend came to tell me about the accident I cried – not for him, but for another delay in freeing us from him. There was no way I could serve him with divorce papers when he was in such critical condition. My conscience would not allow it. But by February it was time to get things rolling again and I did.

Less than a year later we were free. My babies and I continued to live at the apartment in spite of the fact that Todd was absolutely terrorizing us. He would follow me everywhere and attack me verbally or physically whenever he had the opportunity. The restraining order I had on him was worthless. All the police would do was talk to him. One night, however, when he was peering through a small crack in my living room and saw another man inside, he went completely mad. He kicked in the apartment window, shattering the glass into the living room before he ran. He called from a nearby payphone and threatened to tie me to a tree and beat me until I was dead. He came back to the apartment and smashed a bottle against the bedroom window. The babies were screaming. I went to their cribs and tried to calm them, which worked only until he started pounding on the windows and doors. The police were called once again and once again I felt like it was my fault, until they had their encounter with him. After chasing him through several suburban highways they were finally able to stop and apprehend him. At 4 a.m. the phone rang. It was from the officer who responded to the original call. He almost apologetically informed me that they had him in custody. He just wanted me to rest assured.

The only charges brought against him were for criminal damage to property, breaking a window. There were no charges for what he had done to us. But when he was sentenced to six months in the county workhouse I at least felt like I could breathe for awhile.

March 1978. At twenty-one I was divorced and raising two children in diapers by myself and loving it. However it became more and more difficult to find the money to feed them and buy their diapers. There was no one available to look after them so I couldn't work outside the home and consequently became dependent on the welfare system.

During this time and for several months I had debilitating back pain. The only way I could get relief was by taking a prescribed muscle-relaxer. It didn't do much to get rid of the pain, but it did make me care less about it. It gave my whole body a pleasant, calming effect. On my twenty-first birthday I discovered how much better I felt when I mixed it with a little bit of that nasty tasting vodka.

Since the constant pain in my back only seemed to be getting worse, I decided to go to a local chiropractor to see if I could get some relief there. The doctor told me that recovery would require several visits on a regular basis, so every day for the next few weeks I went in for therapy, developing a relationship with him that was becoming more personal. We discussed the miserable divorce I went through while he admitted his was pretty difficult too. Many times I would be his last appointment of the day so we could chat longer and eventually ended up developing more than a doctor-patient relationship. When he confessed that he was twenty-four years older than I it didn't matter because he didn't look his age and he was so nice to me. He had witnessed bruises on my back after one of Todd's assaults so he was very aware of what a lunatic I was dealing with, but we starting dating anyway.

The kind doctor loved children, showing a natural patience with mine. And when Todd went berserk after peeking in my windows that night he was determined to defend us with a hammer, but fortunately the police took care of Todd for us. The doctor stayed in our lives on a regular basis, spending almost every night in bed with me. He showed me what it was like to have someone make love to me. He let the kids know they were safe. This kind and gentle man was different than any I had known.

The back pain seemed to improve with time, but the stress in my life hadn't. So I returned to the medical doctor who had prescribed the painkillers for me, and came home with a prescription for Valium. Soon I discovered that this new medication with a shot of vodka numbed all of my pain, physical and mental. The chiropractor watched helplessly as I destroyed myself with the deadly combination.

Valium and Vodka became a part of my daily diet. The only change in them was the quantity I was taking. Within six months of taking the dangerous cocktails, and compromising the lives of my babies and myself, my doctor and I decided that a treatment program for addicts and alcoholics might be necessary to get me off of them, especially after I shared with him what had happened after I downed a few of my cocktails. During one of our "naps," my babies had managed get out of their cribs. I was awakened to hear them giggling and rushed around the corner to the bathroom where they were about to play with the bubbles they had created in the toilet with my blow dryer. I snatched them away from the toilet full of electrical charge and yanked the cord from the wall before I collapsed on the floor, holding them close and telling them how sorry I was through my tears of guilt and shame.

The doctor recommended that I check into a program as soon as I could make arrangements for someone to look after my kids. He referred me to the county's community services where a homemaker was hired to stay with them for the 28 days I would be away.

Being in a locked facility is an emotionally wrenching experience, especially when you are sharing a ward with a bunch of raving lunatics. It wasn't until three or four days of withdrawal had passed that I was finally allowed onto a ward with the more sane alcoholics. Treatment consisted of the standard meetings, groups, and paperwork day in and day out every day. After almost 30 days at this attempt at brainwashing I couldn't wait to get back home to my kids. It seemed like forever since I had been able to put my arms around them. They felt so good and looked so cute! For some reason they were even cuter than I remembered. It was going to be all right now, I tried to tell them. But at their age all that mattered was that I was home.

Fall 1978. In late September I received a notice from the Housing Authorities saying that I had qualified to occupy a brand new townhouse in a complex that was being built. About a month later we were moving in. It was a beautiful three bedroom split-level town home in "Prestigious West Bloomington" as it was known. Our low-income housing project in this neighborhood appeared out of place in the middle of high-rent apartments and million dollar homes. We were all very excited to have such a huge and bright place, so unlike the dark and musty-smelling, lower-level apartment we had come from.

This had the smell of fresh paint and new carpet. The master bedroom was upstairs while the other bedrooms were downstairs. Jack's bedroom was directly underneath mine, whereas DeAnne's was on the opposite side of the house. Next to her bedroom was another bedroom or den, which had a door to the outside. Over the next many years DeAnne made use of that door more times than I care to remember.

August 1979. Things had spiraled out of control again. Feelings of depression and suicide were normal for me. The only way I felt some relief was with pills and alcohol, which were still being prescribed by unknowing doctors and strange men. After my second in-patient treatment I was assigned a county social worker who checked in on a weekly basis. She was an elderly person with a heart of gold and treated me and the kids as if we were her family. When she saw the direction I was heading she recommended I check into another treatment program. She arranged foster care for my kids, who were now two-and-a-half and three-and-a-half years old and seemed excited to be going on this sleep-over, not understanding why. They were comfortable and happy with the couple they were placed with. They were a bi-racial couple; he was black, and she was white. They had no children but had a comfortable home that seemed very well suited for mine at that time. We hugged, kissed and cried when it was time to say good-bye. That night I sat home and drank until I puked and passed out. The next morning I had a couple of shots before I drove myself to the treatment center.

This twenty-eight day program was shortened by about twenty days. In the short time I was there I knew I was insincere about being there. I just stayed because I felt I had to. When my parents tried to become involved it only ended up in disaster. My dad and I had a huge argument after our differences and similarities collided. My mom ended up in tears feeling as if everything was her fault. A few days later I quit the program and drove myself home. When I first got home I thought I could control my addiction, so I picked up my children and tried, convinced that if I just stayed away from everything, including what the doctors wanted me to take, I would be fine. For about six weeks I didn't drink or take any pills and I didn't like it.

Sometime in early fall I met a man who was ten years older than I was. He was a heavy drug user, who would often pull up in some junker with a pint of brandy in one hand and a joint in another, with his daughter in tow. She was a young girl who hadn't quite reached puberty yet but was very mature for her age. She would watch as her dad would share lines of cocaine with adults who were there in my home. He also handed out something called Quaaludes like they were candy. I liked it all.

By the end of the year the combination of all the drugs I was taking was making me increasingly paranoid. Of course, the fact that I was still being stalked and terrorized by my former husband didn't help. I became nervous and anxious when I had to go out, so I spent most of my time at home, drinking. My social worker noticed that once again I was headed for trouble, so shortly after the holidays she arranged for someone to come and stay with the kids while I checked into a ten-day psychiatric program. The elderly black woman who stayed in our home while I was gone appeared to be a kind and loving person, someone with whom I felt safe leaving my children.

The ten days in the hospital were an opportunity for me to take a break from everything at home and try to get back on my feet again. Even though it was hard to say good-bye to my kids, my alcohol, and my drugs, I knew I needed the time out. At the same time I knew I wasn't serious about not drinking anymore. In fact, when I was given an evening out pass while I was there, I went out and had a few drinks at my favorite hang-out. I thought I was pretty clever in hiding my consumption when I returned to the ward, but the next day I was confronted with the smell and was no longer allowed to leave the premises. Within days of returning home I was sweet-talking one of the men I knew so I could get drunk.

January 1980. My youngest sister seemed concerned about my chemical use until she moved in with us. Weeks after she turned eighteen she moved out of our parents' house, frustrated with the constant arguing between Mom and Dad. So, much to the dismay of our parents, she decided to move in with us during her last year of high school. With her determination, and a little help from my former counselor, she did successfully graduate from high school. Unfortunately, as soon as she did she became more involved in my bad habits. She loved her Bacardi 151 and a joint once in awhile. She also liked to indulge in the "goodies" my friends would share with us. DeAnne and Jack seemed very happy after Penny moved in. She became more than an aunt to them, especially with DeAnne. She became a close friend and part-time mom to both. Everyone seemed to be happy.

February 1980. A little before noon, I was on my way downtown to meet a friend for lunch. Driving down the interstate I suddenly noticed a highway patrol car behind me with its lights flashing. Glancing down at my speedometer I moved over a lane, as did the patrol car until we were both parked on the shoulder of the freeway. As I shuffled through my purse for my driver's license I assumed I was being pulled over for speeding since I did have a bad habit of exceeding the posted limits. It was time I was ticketed, I thought. But as the officer examined my I.D., he said he pulled me over because the rear window in my car was frosted up and he wondered if my vision was obstructed. He asked me to step out of the car and go to his vehicle where he opened the front passenger's side door and asked me to have a seat. He came around to the driver's side and took his seat, his belt and gear creaking as he sat down. He picked up his radio and made contact with someone who informed him that he was holding an individual with a warrant out for her arrest. None of their lingo really made sense to me so it didn't occur to me what was going on until the officer looked at me pathetically and informed me that he would have to place me under arrest. He went on to explain that I had an unpaid parking ticket that I needed to pay before I could be released and that meant a trip to the county jail. He apologized over and over as we sat waiting for my car to be towed.

As we exited the freeway we were stopped at a stoplight. For no apparent reason the officer started waving his arms like he was crazy. I didn't have a clue what he was doing and I wasn't about to ask. After the light changed we drove through the intersection. The officer abruptly pulled to the curb, jammed his car into park, and jumped out of the car. I turned to watch him go to the car behind us and open the driver's door. He grabbed two open bottles of beer and slammed them on the roof of the vehicle that was occupied by three men who appeared to be about my age. I could see the officer having an unfriendly conversation with the men for a few minutes before he returned to the patrol car. He opened his door, handed me the open bottles of beer and politely asked if I would hold them before he got back in. It was then that he explained that all of the men had been drinking and had nearly hit the patrol car from behind at the light. He took their identification cards and told them to follow us. Looking at the beers in my hands I have to confess what a temptation it was to drink them.

We pulled into the underground area of the jail with the other guys behind. The officer was greeted by a female jailer and two other officers, all ready to take in the latest offenders. The woman led me into a small room between two locked doors. She instructed me to place my hands on the large glass window that faced the office area. All of the officers on the other side were men and all of them with their big smiles were very much enjoying their fellow officer feeling this young woman up and down. Rage and fear took over. I could not believe what was happening.

I was led into another area where an Amazonian-type female officer waited. She took me to an area where I was finger-printed and photographed, before I was led down the hall to a small cell with cold grey walls, a stainless steel toilet and sink, and a couple of benches. I sat down and held my head in disbelief. Several hours later the same Amazon came to my cell and unlocked the door. I didn't think I would be happy to see her again, but when she informed me that all I had to do was pay the fine and I could be released, I wanted to hug her. I was able to write them a check and was released a short time later. It was great getting out of that smelly hole and taking a breath of fresh air. Since my car had been impounded my sister and her boyfriend came to pick me up, with a pint of vodka in hand knowing I would need it.

April 1980. It took two years for me to realize the real value of the relationship I had with the chiropractor. One day the good doctor lied to me about his plans to spend that Easter Day with his children. Later on that same day I saw him with another woman. Just prior to the encounter I had stopped by his apartment to slip an Easter card under his door, only to discover that he had moved two weeks earlier and didn't tell me. It made absolutely no sense when we were still sleeping together almost every night. Why would he move and not tell me? Confused and shocked I drove back home in a daze wondering what to do next. The first thing was to slam down a couple of shots of vodka, I knew that much.

Knowing there was a good possibility that he would be at his parents' house, I decided to drive over there. Still I was surprised to see his car parked outside. My heart was racing as I circled the block swallowing one then another shot from the bottle I had stashed in the glove compartment. As I came around the corner the second time I noticed him standing in their doorway as if he was getting ready to leave. Moments later he left the house with his arm around another woman. The blow was too much. After a brief confrontation in the street I got back in my car, insanely driving home at a dangerously high rate of speed. I didn't care. I didn't think I could live with the pain of his betrayal.

The next morning my sister dropped the kids off at their preschool. A short time after they left I swallowed two bottles of tranquilizers and anti-depressants, washing them down with a couple of shots of vodka. Seconds later I panicked and tried to make myself vomit. Then remembering what had happened the night before I changed my mind again and called the good doctor telling him he didn't need to worry about me anymore. For the next few minutes I bounced back and forth between wanting to live and wanting to die. I worried about the effect my death would have on my children, but then I would convince myself that they would be better off without me. About a half hour after I took the overdose the police and an ambulance showed up after receiving a call about a possible suicide attempt. They convinced me to go with them by telling me that I was about to go through some serious discomfort if I didn't. I spent the next three days in the intensive care unit before I was sent home. My mother picked me up when I was discharged. She was waiting in the car just outside the entrance, with DeAnne and Jack in the back seat. As soon as I got in the car she told me how selfish I was. Other than that we never talked about what had happened.

The first thing I did when I walked in the house was fill a small juice glass with the vodka that I had left in the freezer. I took a large gulp, rolling the liquid over my tongue quickly so the bitter taste didn't sink in. I wanted to gag, but I took another swallow instead. Each swallow got easier, especially when my body began to feel wonderfully warm and calm.

When I left the hospital I had a prescription for another kind of tranquilizer and an anti-depressant. Even though the labels in glaring red said not to drink with them, I did. My behavior and judgment dwindled with my increased doses of alcohol and pills. Most nights I would get a babysitter so I could hang out at some of the bars along the strip in Bloomington. It didn't bother me that I was going alone and with no money because I could usually meet some lonely pig who would buy me drinks, oftentimes escorting me home and paying for the babysitter. All I had to do was spend a few hours in bed with them afterwards. If I didn't feel like going out, I never seemed to have a problem getting some guy to come over with a bottle for me. Again all I had to do was spend a few hours in bed with him. Most of my trashy behavior took place when the kids were asleep; otherwise they just thought I had a lot of male friends. And they certainly had no way of knowing that many of these men were married.

Fall 1980. Just before DeAnne turned five I decided to tell her about Paul, the inseminator. It wasn't planned. It just seemed to be the right thing to do at the moment. The kids and I had just driven down to the nearest convenience store to pick up some milk and treats when on the way home I suddenly found myself blurting out the story of her background. I knew from the start I would not keep anything from her. I just hadn't planned on any particular day or time. Both DeAnne and Jack sat in the back seat and listened intently as I told them the story of a little girl who had two daddies. I went on to explain that the little girl had one daddy who helped make her and another one who helped to take care of her (leaving out the fact that they were both losers.) She was developing way beyond her chronological age and understood more than most children her age, so it didn't take long for her to piece the story together. When she asked me if the little girl in the story was her I told her it was. Nothing more was said for several seconds. I tilted the rearview mirror and could see the look of contemplation on their faces. DeAnne continued to ponder the thought. When she said she understood, her brother interjected a "me too" but I knew he really didn't.

Finally she asked me what her other dad looked like. I wanted to say "like a pig." But I only said he had dimples just like hers. When she asked me if he was nice, I wanted to tell her he was a jerk, but instead told her sometimes he was, sometimes he wasn't. She wanted to know if both dads knew about each other. I told her they did, but they didn't like talking to each other.

Meanwhile Todd was continuing with his craziness. Since he signed DeAnne's birth certificate he was legally responsible for her. Consequently, he was forced to make child support payments, and was allowed visitation by the court. It didn't matter that DeAnne was not biologically his. Nor did it matter that he was extremely violent. He still had rights and responsibilities according to the system.

Summer 1982. For awhile most things in my life remained the same. Nothing got worse, and nothing got better. My sick relationships continued and Todd continued to make my life miserable. My drinking and drug use were the same – heavy. When I wasn't at one of my favorite hangouts, I was at home nursing a bottle. Twenty-four hours a day, everyday. Even in the morning I would have a couple of shots before I would take the time to brush my teeth, many times throwing it right back up. But I kept trying until I was able to keep a shot down, then the rest were easy.

One evening when I was at my regular watering hole I met a very handsome, soft-spoken man. When he invited me back to his place my answer was an easy "Yes." He lived alone in a posh townhouse near where I lived. We spent a hot and heavy few hours together and agreed we would get together again soon. Over the next couple of months this very successful and well educated man became less and less available. Since he was a long distance runner and took good care of himself, we didn't really have a lot of the same interests. But I really wanted to have a relationship with him, so I decided to take up running myself. With his advice I started off slowly, walking one block, running the next, until I could gradually increase the running distance. Finally when I was able to run two miles without stopping I called the runner with the good news and asked if we could get together. We met in a nearby park and trotted breathlessly through the trees. I had almost built up the courage to tell him how attracted I was to him when he told me he was getting married. I could not run home fast enough. We never saw each other again. But I continued to run and eventually quit smoking, cold turkey, just so I could run more effectively.

January 1983. After talking to myself for a few months I set a goal to quit smoking cigarettes on the first of January. No one thought I would succeed since I had been smoking at least two packs a day for quite some time. But that New Year's Eve at exactly twelve o'clock I put my last cigarette out. Running had become an addiction and one day after finishing a two mile run I thought of how stupid it was to light up right after doing something so healthy. I read whatever I could in preparation for quitting, so when the time came I was prepared to let go.

Fall 1983. One warm evening I didn't feel like cooking so I decided to take the kids out for a burger. As we stood in line I couldn't help but notice the man standing directly in front of us. He glanced to his left just long enough for me to get a quick look at his profile. His face was very familiar. It couldn't be, I thought, as I connected the face to the "inseminator." He turned around looking for a seat, not noticing the young family behind him. When our dinner arrived I led the kids in the opposite direction of the dining room. Suddenly I had lost my appetite, but poked at my food until I saw him walking toward the exit door right behind the kids' backs. He paused for a moment then pointed at DeAnne as if he was asking about her. I nodded my head. He paused again and then walked out. DeAnne noticed that I was having some kind of communication with someone behind their booth. She turned and exchanged looks with him just before he walked out the door. True to her always curious self, she asked me who the man was. I told her it was Paul. It took a moment for it to register before she looked at me stunned and asked if it was her dad. As soon as I told her it was she pleaded with me to go let her talk to him. She just wanted to meet him. She was becoming very agitated and insistent until I explained that I was afraid he might not be as nice to her as she would like him to be, but we both kept looking, hoping he would come in and at least greet her. She eventually calmed down but pouted about it the rest of the evening.

September 1983. After both DeAnne and Jack were in school full-time I decided to go back to school myself. My social worker was eager to assist in my getting a G.E.D. and pursuing further education. The wheels turned very quickly and within a month or so I had tested for and received my diploma and begun attending a technical college studying electronics. It wasn't a subject I would have picked for myself, but with the results of interest and aptitude tests, I decided to pursue it. The first day of school was exciting and scary, but leaned more toward the scary side when I entered the classroom and found that I was the only female in a class of nineteen. All of the guys in the class welcomed me and treated me as if I was one of them. But the instructor made it clear that he didn't think it was the right place for a female. Regardless of his biased attitude toward me I was able to maintain a 4.0 grade average. But he made it so miserable for me to come to school that I dropped out after almost eighteen months.

August 1984. During the time I was struggling with my instructor I met another student at the school who was studying cabinet making. I had been sitting in the cafeteria working on an assignment when I felt someone looking at me. I looked up toward the pop machine and saw a very attractive man with long dark hair, and a neatly groomed beard and mustache. He smiled at me and nodded his head as if to say "Hi." A few days later we crossed paths again, finding an instant attraction to each other.

In spite of the hurt and betrayal by the doctor, he and I continued to see each other throughout the years. Our relationship had changed however. He used me for sex and I used him for alcohol. He continued to see other women. I continued to see other men. But when I met this handsome man who was much younger and healthier than the doctor, someone who wasn't married and appeared to be attracted to me as a person I fell hard for him, and he for me. We spent every day together in school and after school. We would go out almost every week-end drinking and dancing. The kids loved his energy and humor, but it was obvious he was not as welcoming toward them. It wasn't that he treated them badly; he just wasn't comfortable around kids.

January 1985. Three or four months into my relationship with my schoolmate, the good doctor came up with a surprising invitation. He was going to a chiropractic convention in Hawaii and wanted to know if I would join him. Throughout the years he had talked many times about this fantasy of taking me to Hawaii. His health was failing, which seemed to draw him closer to me. But by now he only repulsed me. However, when he extended the invitation to take a trip I knew I probably would never have the opportunity to take again, I accepted. It wasn't until the night before I left that I broke the news to my new boyfriend. He called the next morning and begged me not to go. But our plans were made. My sister would be looking after the kids part of the time and part of the time they would unfortunately stay with their dad and I was on my way out the door. His voice was soft and sad as he told me he would be waiting for me to get back.

When the doctor arrived to pick me up a few minutes later he looked awful. He was thin and pale, wheezing as he slowly climbed up the stairs. At that moment, I only felt repulsion and compassion. We talked very little on the way to the airport and throughout the flight. When we landed in Honolulu we got off the plane and on the tarmac were greeted by cheerful Hawaiians who placed garlands around our necks and welcomed us to their island. The beauty surrounding us was already breathtaking. Fortunately and unfortunately we did everything very slowly because the doctor was having such difficulty with his breathing, yet refused to seek medical help. When we would travel around the island to look at some of the sights, I would drive while he slept. It had become impossible for him to do much of anything. After several long and worrisome days I begged him to be reasonable and seek some medical attention. His reaction was angry, rude, and defensive. By this time even though it was only halfway through our original plans, I was looking for an opportunity to go back home. His verbal attack did it. I was on the next available flight back to Minneapolis and looking forward to seeing the young, healthy, and attractive man who I knew was waiting for me.

July 1985. For a few years I managed to stay out of hospitals, treatments centers, and jail. That is until about the second week in July when I found more rage in me than I thought possible.

Shortly after I returned from Hawaii I started noticing things that didn't seem quite right when DeAnne and Jack would return from their visits with Todd. DeAnne would often come home with money, clothes, stereo and televisions, while Jack would come home empty handed. After every visit I would observe how they behaved and how they were feeling. My concern had always been that he would hurt one of them, but they both appeared to be very happy about their visits.

DeAnne had had a bedwetting problem from an early age. A doctor recommended that she have exploratory surgery to see if there was something physically wrong with her. It killed me when they wheeled her frightened, little, drugged-up body into the operating room. I sat outside wondering if I had made the right choice. The thought of something going wrong during an exam to stop bedwetting was making me crazy. But it was such a problem for her at night that I felt I had to do something. When the tests came back saying there were no abnormalities I was so relieved, but still concerned about the problem. She also seemed to be having terrible nightmares in which she would often call out, act fitful, and many times wet the bed. The next step was to take her in for a psychiatric evaluation, so I took her to a child guidance center where they gave her a number of tests. In those tests it was discovered that she had a very high I.Q., and that her level of maturity was way beyond her years. Those results really didn't surprise me since it was obvious from an early age that she was bright. Learning came easy to her. Music came easy too. She could sing a song beautifully and play a keyboard without music without effort. The counselors at the children's center recommended I stay aware and involved in her schooling because so often children with her level of intelligence become bored and get into trouble.

Jack was still an innocent and very naïve eight-year-old. He was getting cuter all the time and everyone who met him liked him. He had a serious hearing deficit which forced him to wear hearing aids during the day but at night his sleep was never disturbed by sound. DeAnne's sleep however was very disturbed.

When it seemed appropriate I began asking gentle questions about the goings on at their dad's house while they were visiting. I didn't want them suspicious or fearful of either me or their dad, so I chose my words very carefully. One evening while I was making dinner Jack had wandered through the kitchen when I suddenly found myself asking questions about the visits. How were things going? Was their dad nice to them usually? What were the sleeping arrangements? When he answered the latter I could feel insanity setting in. Casually he told me that he slept on the couch in one room while his dad and DeAnne shared the bed in the other room. My knees weakened and my hands started to shake as he went on to tell me that they had been sharing the bed for awhile. I kissed the top of his head and told him to go and play until dinner was ready. He trotted downstairs and out the door before I flipped out. Screaming at the visions of what he might have done to my poor baby this time, I poured myself a large glass of wine and slammed the cupboard doors until I thought the wood would shatter. Did I want to ask more? Did I want to know more? No, but I had to find out for the sake of my daughter.

While pacing the floor and talking to myself about what I was going to do next, including how I might kill him, DeAnne walked in the door, forcing me to calm down and catch my breath. I went back to the stove and tried to finish dinner, but I couldn't think nor did I care about what was on the stove at that moment. Knowing that I had to be casual with my questioning, I was able to ask her what the sleeping arrangements were during her visits to Todd's. She looked a little frightened like she thought she was in some kind of trouble so I immediately had to find a way to make her more at ease. I told her I was just curious because it had been so long since I had been over to the house he shared with his parents. She nervously told me that she shared the bed with him. When I asked her how she felt about that, she hesitated. She went on to tell me that sometimes it was okay, but other times she felt kind of weird when he would hug her too tight and not let her go. I asked if they all wore pajamas. She told me he wore boxer shorts to bed. I asked if he had ever shown her his privates and when she said yes, I could not bear to hear anymore. She wanted assurance that I would not tell him of the conversation before she went back outside. Not today, was the only honest answer I could give her.

The next day I called my sister, Penny, and told her about the conversation I had with the kids the night before. She knew that I had suspected something like this for several weeks so she wasn't surprised. I told her I needed to confront him right away and asked her if I could meet him in the parking lot where she worked. It was in a semi-public area but by that time of the evening most of the office workers had gone home so the parking area was almost empty. When I called Todd and asked him to meet me I told him it was because my car was making a funny noise and I wanted to know if he could tell me what it was, even though both he and I knew he knew nothing about cars. Penny and I stood in the parking lot talking until we saw his car approach. She agreed to wait for me inside the building. As she walked away I took the six-inch hunting knife from my pocket and opened up the blade, locking it in place. When I saw that face I wanted to strike out at it without hesitation but I waited until he was far enough away from his vehicle that he wouldn't be able to get away easily, just like DeAnne wasn't able to get away. As soon as he realized the real reason for the visit he started ranting, telling me he hadn't done anything. I expected that and followed him back to his car screaming at him that he would never hurt her again. He opened the door to the van he was driving with one hand but turned around and back handed me with the other. The knife came from behind my back and slammed into the arm that had just struck me. The feel of his flesh being cut by the blade of the knife was eerie, but it sunk in without thought or effort on my part. I wanted to hurt him, not thinking of what the consequences of that might be. He threw the van into reverse and tried to back over me as I ran to enter the building where Penny was waiting. Realizing he had missed his target he tore out of the parking lot screaming his usual threats that he would somehow get me back.

As soon as I entered her office, Penny saw the stunned look on my face and the bloody knife in my hand. She listened motionless while I explained what had just happened outside but didn't really have a chance to react before the fear of what he might do to the kids suddenly hit me, especially since I wasn't home. Without waiting for her reaction all I said to her was, "the kids," before I dashed out the door and blindly drove home. The three-mile trip seemed to take forever as terrifying images ran through my mind of what he might do if he reached the house before I did.

My heart raced until I came around the corner and did not see his vehicle anywhere near the house. I ran inside and found both children comfortably focused on the television. Calmly greeting them, I locked the door behind me. They were almost unaware of my presence, thanks to the television, so I went directly to the bathroom, pulled the knife from my pocket and began washing off the bastard's blood. I wrapped it in a rag and buried in under the sink until I was sure I could move it elsewhere without them noticing. Afterwards I went to the kitchen and began to suck down several shots of vodka. By ten o'clock we were all asleep, but sometime around 1 a.m. the phone rang. Still in a drunken daze, I needed several minutes to comprehend what the police officer on the other end was actually saying. He said there had been a report of an assault that I was involved in earlier that evening and asked me if I wanted to explain. I tried to explain everything and must have made some sense because the officer did not feel a need to come over and arrest me right that moment. He said however that I may be charged with a crime because I used a weapon that caused bodily injury. He gave me until the next morning to turn myself in with the knife to answer some questions. The officer sounded very non-threatening over the phone and when he met me the next morning he appeared the same. He shook my hand and thanked me for coming in, and then he escorted me to a small room with a couple of chairs, a table, and a tape recorder. The officer asked permission to turn the recorder on, which made it seem impossible to say, "No." But I knew once he heard what happened and why, he would direct his attention where it was needed – what Todd was doing to his (step)daughter, and drop any possible charges against me. However the county attorney saw it differently and charged me with second degree assault. During the investigation the issue of Todd molesting DeAnne was pursued.

An appointment had been scheduled for a female investigator to come to our house and interview DeAnne and me. DeAnne was nervous and afraid that the police officer would get her in trouble somehow. I wrapped my arms around her and tried to convince her that it would be all right, while envisioning what I wanted to do to the bastard who was doing this to her. At the last minute an officer called and informed me that the incident was being handled by another jurisdiction and consequently it would be a male officer coming over to interview DeAnne. It seemed like a bad idea, but we had no choice if I wanted the prosecutor to understand why I did what I did. Things only got worse when the investigator was a large, hostile man in a business suit who reamed the poor child as if he were interviewing a murderer. She was terrified. In attendance at the interview was a social worker from the county's child protection program. I had also hoped for some support there and again was disappointed when the worker turned out to be a recent immigrant from somewhere in Asia who spoke, and understood, very little English. Both DeAnne and I felt helpless and hopeless. After they left she was so upset that she swore she would never tell anyone again if something happened – not even me.

About a week after the assault took place an officer called to inform me that a warrant had been issued for my arrest and that I had until 7 a.m. the next morning to turn myself in and appear in court on the charges. I couldn't believe what I was hearing! After all of the sick and terrible things that Todd had done to me, to us, how could it be that I had to go to jail?

I called a friend to ask for a ride to the jail before I went to the cupboard. The only way I felt I could cope with what was about to happen was by pouring myself a couple of shots of vodka and washing them down with a can of diet cola. I mixed a few pretzels in so I wouldn't show up with a sick and empty stomach. What was about to happen was making me sick enough. Nothing would come as a surprise, I thought, because I had been through the incarceration process before. But this time was no less humiliating and degrading as the female officer ordered me to place my hands up against the wall and spread my legs. Silent tears washed over my face, rage ran through my blood. The hefty female officer led me to a small room and ordered me to hold a numbered sign, stand on a black mark on the floor, face left, front, and right. Then she told me to follow her to the table where she would press my fingertips into a black ink-covered sponge before contorting each one onto an identification card. After that she led me to a small cell where I waited for a few hours before I was called to appear in court. When it was time an officer came to my cell and told me to put my hands behind my back. He locked each handcuff tightly around my wrists, and then told me to follow him. I appeared very out of place when I was led to an elevator where several black males in jail garb with their hands cuffed behind their back were already waiting. Their vulgar and frightening stares made me wish I could just disappear, especially when we were all loaded onto the same elevator with a couple of officers to the courtroom. When my case was called one of the officers removed my handcuffs before the public defender met with me in front of the judge. I made a routine "not guilty" plea, was assigned another court date, then led back to the waiting area where the handcuffs were locked back on and the harassment of the other offenders continued.

The judge allowed me to leave without bail, so after a few hours of waiting for paperwork to be processed I was set free. Since I went into jail with nothing I came out with nothing and had no idea what I was going to do, so after several very deep breaths of fresh air I walked a few blocks to where a friend worked and got a ride home. On the way home we stopped at the first liquor store we came to so I could get a few shots in me before I got there. As soon as I walked in the door I wrapped my arms around my babies and told them how happy I was to see them.

About a month later another hearing was scheduled at which time Todd was also to be charged with assault for striking me and using his van to try to run over me. He never showed up and after several minutes in the courtroom it was decided that all of the charges against me would be dropped. However it would give me little satisfaction since at the same time the investigation involving DeAnne and her stepdad would also be dropped. All I could do was keep a close eye on her before and after the visits for signs that something may still be going on. Whether something was happening or not, she was very guarded about sharing anything that went on during the visits for the next several years.

Fall 1985. One Sunday morning while the kids were on a routine visit at their dad's, I went to visit a friend who was always good for a drink, some weed, and some cocaine and I wanted them all. I knew he would expect a piece of me in return and at the time I was willing to let him have me just so I could get totally screwed up before I had to go home. Everything went as I had expected it to except for the ride home. About three miles before I was to reach my destination there was an area of the road that was dark, curvy, and under construction. As I drifted through the quarter mile section of road I felt several bumps and thumps, and crunches, and dragging sounds before the road smoothed out again. Ignoring the terrible sound coming from the rear end of my car I decided as long as the car was still moving I was going to keep moving, regardless of what I was dragging. I pulled into the driveway at home and parked the car in the garage. After safely getting it inside I looked at the back end where the noise had been coming from and found my rear bumper laying on the ground with severe damage to the entire rear end of my car. My license plate was also missing, so the next day as soon as I could get a ride I returned to the area of the accident and found several signs downed, tire tracks on either side, with metal car parts and strips strewn everywhere. I was frightened and embarrassed by the damage I had done and only vaguely remembering doing it. My license plate was never recovered, but no charges were ever filed against me.

August 1986. Meeting men was never a problem for me, but occasionally I would agree to a blind date just for fun. One invitation was to meet a man from Italy. Since I had never known anyone from Italy I was intrigued. We agreed to meet at a restaurant in South Minneapolis where I knew it would be quiet and quaint (and where they served alcohol). I arrived way before the scheduled time so I could down a few Black Russians first. About half way through my third I noticed a homely little man come in the door. He was wearing a brown wool suit, white socks, and brown wingtip shoes. He was almost bald and his complexion looked like he had suffered serious acne since he was a child. The matchmaker told him what I looked like but did not tell me what he looked like so I had no idea what to expect, but he was not the vision of the Italian Stallion that I had hoped to be meeting.

The interesting thing about Georgio was that he was the kindest, most generous person I had ever met. It was impossible not to be attracted to him immediately because of his soft Italian voice and childlike persona as he was trying so hard to communicate. He would often pull out what he referred to as his "bible" to translate, and was able to quickly catch on to the English language. And like so many others, he was married.

Every year for several years he would travel from Milan to Minneapolis once or twice for 30 to 60 days for training in telecommunications. We would spend as much time as possible together when he visited, in a very unusual relationship. We cared very much about each other, and he was kind to me and my children. After a few years he invited me to visit his hometown in Italy. It was clearly an opportunity that most women aren't offered every day so it took a lot of thought and consideration for a few years. An all expense paid trip to Europe, leaving two young children that I felt I could not trust to anyone. I felt I could not live with myself if I left on the trip and something happened to one of them, but I kept dreaming.

October 5, 1986. Regardless of the dangers and warnings from different doctors I continued to take anti-depressants, major tranquilizers, and other anti-psychotic medication to help with my serious bouts with depression and thoughts of suicide. Most days were spent finding someone to visit me with plenty of alcohol and/or weed. A combination of Quaaludes or cocaine was always nice too while the kids were at school. By the time they got home I was usually in the same state of inebriation. My "state" became so normal to them that they had no idea how much alcohol or what drugs I consumed during the day. Many times my head was already hanging over the toilet before they even got home.

One day after the kids had left for school, still feeling the effects of the drunk the night before, I made myself a strong screwdriver. My stomach was churning but I knew I had to eat something so I gagged down a piece of toast and made myself a second orange juice cocktail. The night before I had fallen asleep feeling very depressed about my situation to the point that I wondered once again if DeAnne and Jack would be better off without me. As the morning progressed the same thoughts consumed me and intensified to the point that I was afraid of myself. The thought of taking another handful of pills and going to sleep was so strong, but the voices of my kids were just as loud. Thinking that maybe if I talked to somebody about what was going on, and how I was feeling, these ideas would go away, I picked up the phonebook and called the suicide prevention line listed in the front. The person who answered the phone seemed genuinely concerned and wanting to help when I explained my desperation to her.

After several minutes of conversation the woman asked if I would be willing to drive to the intervention center about 15 miles away. Not having disclosed the fact that I had consumed a couple of screwdrivers along with a couple of shots of vodka, I picked up my keys and drove to the crisis center.

The kind voice met me at the entrance and asked me to follow her into a small office area and down a short hallway with several small rooms on each side. She escorted me into one of the rooms, closed the door and asked me to sit down. Then she asked for my keys and left the room. She came back a few moments later and asked me to follow her. Confused, but still wanting to talk, I followed her – right into another locked cell. As soon as she got me inside she turned around, then shut and locked the door. I sat down on the edge of the cot, holding my face and sobbing, wondering what I had gotten myself into, when the door opened again and two men in white uniforms came in and informed me that I was going for a ride. They escorted me down the short hallway, ignoring my tears and questions. With one man on each side I was helped onto their waiting ambulance. Nothing was making any sense and no one was saying anything. The woman who had welcomed me had disappeared.

One of the men climbed into the back of the ambulance and asked me to lie down on the gurney. He seemed kind enough but he seemed unable to hear any of my questions as he strapped me in. The only thing he did say was that I was on my way to the county's detox center. Within minutes we were backing into a small brick building. The driver came around and opened the back door while the other one unbuckled me and signaled me to exit. We walked directly inside the building and heard the loud clank of the steel doors locking shut behind us. The two men handed me off to a man and woman dressed in street clothes. They too seemed to be deaf. They led me to an office area and began the standard intake questions. When I refused to answer any of their questions until they told me why I was there, a silent communication took place between a few of the office personnel who snatched me out of my chair and physically escorted me down a hallway of small cells. It was possible to see into each cell because of the long narrow windows in each locked door. Each one was occupied by a man who appeared to be drunk or sleeping one off.

They opened a door near the end and instructed me to enter the dingy cell, immediately locking the door behind me without saying anything. It had to be a nightmare! All I did was wake up feeling very depressed and all of a sudden I found myself locked in a little padded cell with a only a 4 x 6 mat and a plastic bottle for a toilet. All I could do was sit in the corner and sob, wondering what I had done that suddenly I was being treated as if I were a criminal. Several obviously drunk or hung over males, most of whom were Native Americans, wandered by the cell as soon as word got out that there was a young, attractive white female in there. After several hours a woman came in and instructed me to follow her. Rather than ask any more questions of another set of deaf ears I just followed her. She led me to a room with several beds and said someone would be in to talk to me shortly. She pointed to an open bed near the window. A few hours later another woman who seemed to be more sensitive and talkative came into the room and called my name. The alcohol buzz I had going earlier was wearing off. My hands were beginning to shake and I felt nauseous. Later in the afternoon I was allowed to call my sister and ask her to look after the kids and try to make up something about where I was. Once again she covered for me.

The night dragged on, leaving me sleepless. The only thing to occupy my mind was the neon clock across the freeway. All night I sat up and stared at the clock, wondering what I had done wrong. Early the next morning the soft spoken woman came into the room and asked me to join her at the main desk to fill out paperwork. Not wanting to give anyone any reason to keep me any longer, I answered anything she asked. While I was sitting there I noticed a brochure that said something about patient rights. Before I left her desk I asked for a copy and took it back to my room. The brochure gave me exact instructions on how to file a grievance. As soon as I finished reading it, I went back out to the main desk, asked for a paper and pen, and began writing. I briefly explained to the person in charge of the appeal that I was extremely depressed and just wanted to talk to someone when I found myself at the detox center. Thirty minutes after giving my letter to the soft-spoken one I was told an ambulance was on the way to take me back to the crisis center.

When we arrived the same woman was there and led me to the same office as before and asked me why I was there, as if the eighteen hours in between hadn't happened. Livid and despising her I told her I had nothing to say except that if I ever felt suicidal again I would know better than to call her for help. She handed me my keys and told me I was free to leave. As soon as I got home I poured myself one shot after another, not wanting to share the miserable and humiliating experience with anyone.

Spring 1987. For several months I had been seeing a doctor about problems I was having with my stomach. It was understandable that I was vomiting as much as I was, considering how much alcohol I was consuming daily. The liquor would numb my appetite, so I just kept drinking on an empty stomach, and vomiting alcohol, bile, and blood. Mouthfuls of blood. I tried to keep everything from everyone by running the sink faucet or shower, and keeping it all a secret. No one knew that my doctor had already told me six months earlier that if I didn't quit drinking it would kill me. Sometimes I would disregard what he said as justification for an indirect way of committing suicide.

When it got to the point that I could not eat or drink anything but milk and soda crackers (in between shots, of course), the doctor said that I had developed several issues related to my upper G.I. area. The only option to control my symptoms was surgery. He explained the risks and the rewards. The thought of being able to eat or drink anything without discomfort or vomiting far outweighed any risk so I had the surgery in mid-summer. Outside of general recovery from the surgery I only felt relief. However, the doctor made it perfectly clear that I had to avoid alcohol. With that in mind I joined an outpatient treatment program for women.

Twice a week for several months I faithfully attended the meetings mainly because I had developed an especially close relationship with my counselor. She was so supportive and compassionate. For about a year my respect for her kept me sober.

Summer 1988. Although I had made the decision to start drinking again I talked myself out of the guilt and shame of it by reducing the percentage of alcohol I was consuming in a day, switching to boxes of wine instead of bottles of hard liquor, but smoking more weed with my glasses of wine. It was readily available since I was growing several healthy plants for a friend who in turn offered me quite a bit of his profit. We had the setup in the room next to DeAnne's with the back door. There was a large cone-shaped aluminum shade and floodlight going constantly, leaving a strong skunky smell throughout the house. My neighbors didn't care what I was doing, and I was "close friends" with the married landlord who provided alcohol whenever I needed it and looked the other way regarding the illegal activities going on in my rental unit.

It was almost midnight one Sunday when it occurred to me that I had forgotten to put the clothes that I had planned to wear to work the next day in the dryer. On the way downstairs I noticed DeAnne's door was slightly ajar so I peeked inside and noticed that she had the covers pulled up over her head. It seemed strange since it was such a warm evening, so I asked her if she was cold. When she didn't answer I went to the side of her bed. As soon as I placed my hand on what I thought was her shoulder, I realized there was only a pile of carefully placed blankets where my daughter should have been.

A swell of mixed emotions came over me at once - disbelief, fear, rage, worry, confusion, questions spinning in my head. Where would I start looking for her? Did she leave on her own? How far ahead of me was she? Would I ever see her again?

For several months she had been showing signs of independence and belligerence, acting out at school and at home. She would not do her homework and her straight A's were dropping. She would not come home when she was supposed to or be where she said she was going to be, so I thought it most likely she left on her own and positioned the blankets herself.

After pacing the floor for several minutes, I looked in Jack's room and found him sound asleep, then turned around and noticed the back door was open slightly. Quickly I walked over to it, flipped on the back light and bolted into the backyard when DeAnne suddenly appeared around the corner of the building. She froze in her steps, the color washing from her face as soon as our eyes connected. It was clear she was high by her bloody red and narrowed eyes. My instincts were to hug her and beat the daylights out of her at the same time. Not wanting to wake the neighborhood or Jack my voice was almost silent but deadly as I grabbed the back of her shirt and escorted her upstairs to the living room. After spitting a few words at her it was clear that my ranting was going nowhere. Knowing that as high as she was there was no communicating with her, I postponed any discussion or discipline until the following morning. In a way it was hard to be angry when I knew where she had gotten the weed. The shame I felt for leaving all of that marijuana exposed to my kids made it impossible to enforce any consequences when it was I who was in the wrong. The next day I called the owner of the plants and told him they needed to be removed immediately, but before they were I made sure I had several bags stashed away.

Fall 1988. During DeAnne's elementary school years she consistently received the same report cards. Straight A's came to her with no effort. Her musical ability and singing voice were magical. But from preschool on up, during parent-teacher conferences the teachers would also comment about her inability to keep friends and her habit of fabricating stories. Her first grade teacher said that DeAnne had her absolutely convinced that she had family who were royalty over in England. I don't know how she did it, but she had an uncanny ability to lie to anyone about anything, which made it difficult for her to maintain relationships with other students.

Her first report card in middle school told me there was something wrong. There were no A's. The comments from the teachers were more negative than positive. She was becoming a behavior problem in class and eventually ended up in the school's detention room. During her second year in middle school things only got worse. Even though I encouraged the teachers to call me with any problem they might be having with the kids, the almost-daily negatives reports were becoming a worry and a nuisance. When I would question DeAnne about the decline in her grades or the behavioral issues, she would deny there was a problem until I would get so frustrated trying to understand it that we would just end up in a verbal battle with each other.

When DeAnne and Jack returned to school I started working as a home health aide. At first it worked out well for me because I could pick out my days and hours for the most part, therefore I could be home when or shortly after they would get home. But in the first year of work I had been called several times by teachers regarding problems they were having with DeAnne. Since Jack had been diagnosed with a significant hearing loss, wearing hearing aides for several years, it was also necessary for me to participate in much of the special needs education that he had. It was a strain, but at least I had the flexibility to go to the school when they needed me.

My consolation during those stressful days was in knowing I would come home to a cold beer or glass of wine and a joint. The combination of problems with the kids, alcohol, and hangovers eventually took its toll on my attendance at work so I was forced to cut back more and more, which unfortunately left me with a lot of spare time to sit around and drink while I waited for the next phone call from school.

Winter 1988. One evening while I was upstairs watching television I heard what sounded like a tape playing downstairs. The voice was so angelic yet solid and clear. I turned the television down and quietly walked down the stairs where I could hear the sound of "Over the Rainbow" coming from DeAnne's room. It was a voice I had never heard before, not like that. Quietly, I approached her bedroom door and stood with silent tears streaming down my face. When she finished I slowly opened the door. At first she was alarmed by my tears, but when she realized what they were for she blushed. Embarrassed, she disregarded my request for an encore performance, but from that moment on I kept after her to record the song for me. Finally, I was able to bribe her by allowing a sleepover and she taped it with the help of her piano teacher at school. He knew of her magical voice and was supportive of my request.

One day DeAnne told me she was staying after school to tape the song for me. Since she would need a ride home afterward I left early to pick her up in hopes that I would be able to catch a little of the performance live. As soon as I opened the door to the music auditorium my eyes watered with pride. She sounded so incredibly beautiful with no effort. The music teacher agreed. After finally getting the recording I had wanted so badly, I borrowed one of the kids' boom boxes and carted it around everywhere I went sharing the song with anyone who would sit still long enough to listen to it. And every time I cried. A few months later DeAnne wanted to tape a song from the radio so she plopped "my" tape in and taped over her singing. I was heart-broken and she knew it, so when

I asked her over and over to tape it for me again I really thought she would, but she never did.

DeAnne's incredible beauty, amazing voice, and high level of intelligence had me convinced that she could do anything she wanted. As she went through her adolescent years she went from a cute little girl with green eyes and dimples, to a naturally beautiful young lady. She was tall and slender and let her dark blonde hair grow out past her shoulders. When she was about two she had developed a problem with her hair, losing clumps in various places on her scalp. But as she grew older her hair grew in thick like mine, but blonde and straight like "the inseminator." She had suddenly become taller than me with a very lean figure. Wherever we went people would notice her. Men of all ages would ogle the two of us. The stares were not something unfamiliar to me because I was about the same age as DeAnne when my looks became dangerously tempting to all types of men. It was scary to watch how they looked at her. Sometimes if they looked a little too long the Mother Hen in me would get all ruffled up until the men would catch sight of her possessive mother. After introducing me to her first few boyfriends she said to me, "Mom, all of my boyfriends think you're crazy!" because I was so protective. My answer to that was, "Good."

It frightened me to let her go to her stepfather's house, but she would insist on going. If I didn't allow her, she would make week-ends miserable for me with an angry and pouty attitude. The only reason she would say she wanted to go was because he would buy her things. The things I couldn't afford.

I kept telling myself if there were a problem she would tell me. But the memory of her saying she would never tell again if he did anything to her haunted me every minute she was there. Since he paid child support for both DeAnne and Jack, I was court ordered to allow visitation rights as long as the visits took place at his parents' house, where he lived at the time. Knowing his parents were there gave me some comfort; however, I was fully aware that much of the time they would choose to put their blinders on to a lot of things he did. All I could do was let DeAnne know that I loved her and would do anything to keep her safe. Up to this point she still was not aware of the stabbing and I felt no need to tell her.

Summer 1989. A few weeks after school let out DeAnne tried the old "stuff the bed" trick again and snuck out the back door. Again panic and rage deterred any rational thinking. Should I go looking for her? Where would I start? Should I just wait for her to come home? Should I call the police? When she hadn't returned by early the next morning that's exactly what I decided to do. It would also be the first of many "runaway" police reports I would file. During the day I called all of her friends, none of whom were willing to share her whereabouts with me if they knew anything, so all I could do was wait.

Finally I got a call from her stepfather. She had decided to call him for a buffer before facing my wrath. Not only did it only make me angrier, but it was confusing for me trying to figure out how she could run to this man who I was positive was still up to no good. In the middle of my screaming fit with DeAnne she handed the phone to Todd. She had him believing that I was a raving lunatic and that she was too terrified to come home. When they heard me say that I had already called the police so she needed to come home and that it was safe for her to come home neither of them had a comeback. We hung up but before she stepped in the front door I called the police and let them know that my runaway daughter was home safe.

Every high-volume word that came out of my mouth fell on deaf ears, whether they made sense or not. It got to the point where I had to have bed-checks every night before I could sleep. Sometimes I would wake up in the middle of the night and have to check on her before I could go back to sleep. I tried everything to keep her in the house, even taking all of her shoes in the winter, but nothing would stop her if she wanted to get out. I had installed a lock on the back door that needed a key to get out, put a motion detecting floodlight in the back yard, and rigged her window so I could see if she went out during the night. But she always found a way to leave, even when it meant running through the snow without shoes or boots on to meet her friends. (She would confess later that she just put several pairs of socks on.) She broke so many screen windows that I finally decided to just leave the back door open.

Summer 1990. Over and over I would call the police and report her missing just so they could keep an eye out for her. When an officer recommended family counseling I decided to look into it. The school counselors were also recommending it because of the problems they were still having with her – screaming at teachers, skipping out of school, grades dropping from straight A's to straight F's. We had a few sessions at a Family Center near our home. The young man who counseled us seemed too young to have much experience so I don't think he was ready for us.

During one of DeAnne's disappearing acts we had a scheduled appointment with Gary, our family counselor, during which he admitted having seen her at a coffee shop near his apartment the day before. At first my blood began to boil at the thought that this guy knew where my daughter was and didn't bother to call and tell me. When he saw my reaction he apologized, saying he really didn't know what to do since he was off duty. After much thought, he admitted, he decided to do nothing. He knew I was looking for her even though he recommended that I stop. He felt that my looking for her had become a hide-and-seek game with her, which he said was not healthy. He may have been right, but nothing was going to stop me from looking for my daughter whether he approved or not.

As soon as I left the appointment I drove down to the coffee shop where Gary said he had last seen her. I didn't expect to find her there, but I did want to drop off a picture of her so if she came in again they could call me or the police. I opened the old screen door to the tiny café on the corner, a little bell announcing me. Everyone turned to see who came in, including my daughter. That look of sheer panic drained her face again. She was sitting at a little round wooden table in the corner with a man who was obviously much older that she, probably in his late twenties. Putting myself uncomfortably close to the two of them I asked the man if he knew she was only fifteen years old. She tried to cover her tracks by correcting me, saying she was sixteen. Leaning closer to the man, my eyes bulging and voice frighteningly calm, I told him that I was her mother and that I knew how old she was.

I grabbed DeAnne by the shoulder of her sweater, twisting it out of shape in my fist, accidentally slamming the jingly door against the brick wall on the way out. My car was parked right outside and I did not want her to get away so I held my grasp tightly until I got her into the back of my two-door where she would not be able to escape. I turned the key to the ignition and rolled up the windows before the screaming, spitting, nonsense came out of my mouth until I was hoarse. Since the police had put a warrant out for her for being a runaway again, I decided that this time I would let them handle her, so I drove directly to the police station and parked outside the police entrance until I saw two officers walking up the sidewalk. DeAnne pleaded with me to take her home, but I had already made up my mind - not this time.

The officers listened intently while I explained the situation. Moments later one went to each side of the car and ordered her to get out. She looked terrified as they put the handcuffs on her and led her into the station. Underneath all of the anger that was still raging inside me, I felt my heart breaking. I wanted to take her in my arms, bring her home, and believe that she would stay there, but I knew if I didn't do something drastic things would only get worse. She told me several times that she was not running away from home, but that she just wanted to go party with her friends, like she thought that would make a difference.

After they processed her at the city's police station, she was transported to the county's juvenile detention center where she would spend the week-end. Since I had been at that same detention center many years ago I knew what it was going to be like for her and it tore me up inside. She called as often as they allowed, crying and pleading with me to let her come home but at that point it was out of my hands. When she appeared in court the judge put her on probation with instructions to obey the legal curfew and continue with family counseling. It seemed like a waste of breath because there was nothing up to that point that would keep her indoors at night. Why did he think telling her to follow a curfew would help? And our family counselor had decided that there was nothing more he could do to help us. So that ended that relationship. And nothing changed.

June 1991. Throughout the last few years my Italian friend, Georgio, continued to visit and suggest that some day I visit his homeland. Finally, in May the ticket came in the mail for a ten-day round trip in Italy and the surrounding countries, beginning in Germany. Even though it all seemed like a dream I started making arrangements for the kids immediately. My sister and Todd both agreed to take charge. Of course Todd was not my preferred choice but DeAnne kept insisting that she would be all right. She also promised that she would behave.

The trip had me feeling as if I was living a fantasy and a nightmare at the same time. Aside from my appreciating the experience and the sights of other countries, it was not a trip I thoroughly enjoyed. While I was staying at one of the five-star hotels in Milan, the desk clerk managed to secure the lock on my door so that he was the only one who could open it. When he escorted me back to my room to "help" he also offered to bring me a glass of wine. His English was difficult to understand, but I understood wine. He came back a few minutes later carrying a beer mug full of white wine in one hand and a small glass of wine in his other. He said I appeared sad and lonely and asked if he could come in and share some wine with me. Since it was the middle of the night, he explained, he locked the front door, which would allow him to leave the front desk. Feeling a little lonely, since Georgio had to go home to his wife, I agreed to let him in. With the little English that he knew he kept repeating what a beautiful "Madonna" he thought I was. But as he ran his hand across the top of my strapless dress I knew I was in trouble. He would not take his hands off me, until I threatened to call Georgio. He left the room with an insincere apology. The problem I had at that point was I had no idea how to call Georgio or the police. In the morning as soon as I told Georgio what had happened he moved me to a different hotel.

When it came time for me to leave Italy I was ready. When I got to the airport I felt as if I couldn't board fast enough, but a few minutes before the flight was to take off the air traffic controllers went on strike, which unbeknownst to me occurred often in Italy. My departure was delayed another miserable day. Georgio stayed with me all day and night. How he explained it to his wife I had no clue. It didn't really matter to me anyway. I just wanted to go home.

When I finally arrived back in the states my sister and kids were there to greet me. All of the angst I felt when leaving them was finally gone when I got to put my arms around them. The breaks I took from them always felt good, but seeing them again always felt good too. That evening DeAnne and Jack were on their best behavior since they hadn't seen me for ten days. But the happiness was short-lived when DeAnne handed me a note the next morning before she took off with some of her friends.

The note said that she had gotten into some trouble while I was gone and that she knew I would find out eventually but was afraid to tell me to my face. My stomach started to knot as I continued to read. Apparently, sometime after I left, DeAnne got hold of my car keys, which I left with my sister. One evening when she went out with friends they returned to our empty home and my car. At some point she decided to take my car for a little joy ride. During the course of this excursion she hit a car and a pole, causing some damage to my car. My pulse raced as I folded the note back up and walked out to the garage. There was my little Skyhawk, the newest and best car I had ever owned, banged up and dented in various spots.

I was so angry it was without a doubt a good thing she was not around. After examining the car I went back in the house and called the police. I told them that my daughter had stolen my car and had been in an accident. By the time they arrived DeAnne had returned, so we all had a chat while she walked around the car and pointed out the dents, explaining where they came from as if they were pieces of artwork she had done. Before losing control I asked the officers to deal with her and I went for a walk. When I decided not to press charges they gave her a verbal warning.

Several weeks had gone by and it seemed like DeAnne was really trying to behave. As much as I wanted to believe that she was going to change, I still checked on her every night before I went to bed. One night during a stretch when we were getting along great we had said our usual, 'Good-night, I love you," like we had every night. Some time later she came upstairs to get a drink of water. She came into my bedroom and told me once again that she loved me then she went back to her room. A few hours later the phone rang. It was the Bloomington police. The officer asked if I had a daughter named DeAnne. Then he told me that he had arrested her for driving without a license and driving under the influence of alcohol. I told him there must have been a mistake, but he insisted. Still not believing what he was saying, I ran downstairs to her bedroom and found it empty.

Since he woke me from a sound sleep at 1:00 in the morning I was too woozy to really comprehend what he was saying. He said he noticed a vehicle swerving back and forth down the street so he decided to stop it. The car ran up on the curb before it came to a stop. Inside he found DeAnne behind the wheel of her friend's car smelling of alcohol. I was so angry and fed up I told him to keep her there, but he said the jail was full and that it was not a good place for her to be. I continued to refuse until he threatened to charge me with child abandonment. When I kept refusing to come and get her he said he would take her to a psychiatric hospital in Minneapolis, but he still needed me to meet him there to sign the admission papers. Two hours later in the middle of the night I was driving downtown instead of to the jail a few miles away, trying to make sense of what had happened. DeAnne went through a brief psychiatric evaluation where it was decided that she was not a candidate for commitment. So after signing papers we walked out of the hospital sometime after 3:00 a.m. And again I put her in the back seat of the car and screamed until I was hoarse. I didn't know what to do with her anymore.

Summer 1992. During one of DeAnne's excursions I was once again reminded of my terror years and what I put my parents through. One morning I went downstairs and found her gone, this time not bothering to position the pillows. The same feelings rushed through my veins. How could she keep doing this to me, knowing how worried I'd get, and knowing that she would be punished?

This time after I made the usual rounds of calls to her friends, checking to see if anyone knew where she was, someone leaked that she went to Duluth with a friend. After a few more calls I found out that she decided to go visit some relatives of a friend of hers. They had taken the Greyhound there, and were planning to take the bus back after the get-together. With the help of the bus company, the Duluth police and the St. Paul police, we were once again able to intercept her plans and take her to jail.

First I had to confirm that she was actually in Duluth and planning to take the bus home. Then I had to confirm the time and the fact that she actually boarded the bus. An officer from the Duluth police agreed to get on the bus and look around. I gave him a description of her and told him he would know for sure if she had a small peace sign tattooed on the back of her right wrist, which she had burned in herself several months earlier.

The officer was able to confirm her presence with the tattoo. He called me back and asked if I wanted to come and get her or if I wanted her to take the bus home. When they told me there would be a stop in St. Paul before returning to Minneapolis I decided to meet the bus at the St. Paul depot, just to make sure she didn't get off early. Jack and I went together and met the St. Paul police shortly before the bus arrived to discuss the situation and the plan to retrieve her and make the trip back to the juvenile detention center. The officer would get on first, followed by me, then Jack, who was looking forward to the entertainment of his sister getting busted again.

The officer was tall enough and the backs of the seats were high enough that DeAnne could not see me until I was standing right in front of her. She and her friend were having a grand old time, laughing and sipping on their pop, until they saw me. The laughing faces turned to stone. The officer harshly asked DeAnne to stand up and come with him. Neither Jack nor I said a word. She looked shocked, embarrassed, and frightened as the officer spun her around and slapped his handcuffs on her. A flood of tears was forming in the back of my throat, but I tried to be tough as he closed the back door of the police car behind her and drove off. Once they disappeared around the corner I could not hold the tears back any longer. As soon as we got back to the car Jack reached in the glove compartment and handed me the pint of vodka I had purposely left there, knowing I was going to need a shot after the encounter. All the way back to the house I drove with the pint safely tucked between my legs, occasionally swallowing burning gulps until half of it was gone by the time we got home.

DeAnne called as soon as she was allowed again, and again sobbed on the other end begging me to get her out of there. It hurt so much, but I couldn't. Once again it was up to the courts, but not much had changed. She was still on probation and expected to follow a few more worthless guidelines. It all came back to me protecting her from herself. Occasionally I would feel so desperate that I would want to call "the inseminator" to help me, but when it came right down to it I knew that was asking for a whole new set of problems. DeAnne was still my baby at sixteen and I intended to do whatever I had to in order to keep her safe.

While she was attending junior high school DeAnne's grades and behavior continued to deteriorate. One afternoon I received a call from her counselor asking to meet with me regarding her absences. That made no sense since she left for school and came home on the bus every day. Rage drove me to the school immediately. When I arrived I was escorted into a conference room inside the main office. (It felt strange to be the parent in the office this time.)

There on the table was a file with DeAnne's name on it. While waiting for the counselor I opened the folder and found several notes in DeAnne's handwriting asking to be excused from school for a number of clever and bogus reasons. And they were all "signed" by me. It was a good thing she was not in school right then because I would have hunted her down. Instead I went home and waited.

She walked in the door that afternoon with her usual "hi, Mom," and a peck on the cheek. As soon as she saw the look in my eyes her smile vanished. She knew she was in trouble. When I asked her where she had been all day her famous song and dance started. Since she was old enough to be creative she told stories – lies – constantly.

When her performance ended I held back on the applause but chose instead to slap her several times and demand that she stop lying and tell me where she was. She insisted she was in school to the point that I think she believed it herself. I was so frustrated, exhausted, and out of control I had to let her go before we got into a real battle. Before she left the room, however, I let her know that I had been at the school and informed of the forged notes. From that point on the school was to call me immediately if she was not in school. The phone rang almost every day.

Every year I had accepted the responsibility of attending the parent-teacher conferences. But between Jack's hearing disability and all of the learning and behavioral problems that accompanied it, along with DeAnne's delinquent behavior, it had become such a negative experience that it usually took me a couple of shots of courage before going. All of the teachers had only bad things to say and when I got really tired of hearing it I quit attending altogether.

September 1992. Throughout the summer DeAnne kept reminding me that because she was sixteen she did not legally have to attend school anymore. It was hard to argue the point since I was a dropout, a student who hated school, caused trouble when I was there, and got straight F's too. The difference with her was that she was so intelligent. School never took much effort for her. I had always believed that she failed because she was bored, unlike me who was bored because I had trouble learning and concentrating. It was no surprise when only a few weeks into her sophomore year she quit going. She kept spending more and more time away from home. Finally I had to surrender any hope that she would be safe.

Mother's Day 1993. As DeAnne matured, which was very quickly, she began spending more and more time with people who were older than she was. It didn't surprise or bother me when she brought home male friends who were five or six years her senior. Besides, my prejudice would be hypocritical with my having dated a man 24 years my senior; my feelings were that age did not matter as long as the men were nice to her. During this growing period for both DeAnne and I we became better and better friends. Oh, we'd have some real doozies occasionally about her coming and going as she pleased, but mostly we grew closer.

DeAnne started working at a pizza parlor at the age of fifteen. She loved having her own money, especially since I really never had any to give her. This Mother's Day, like every other gift-giving holiday over the last few years, I asked DeAnne not to worry about buying me a gift. I told her again and again that what I really wanted was for her to re-record her version of "Over the Rainbow." I didn't get it.

What I did receive was something just as beautiful and priceless as her voice. She had folded a small sheet of notebook paper and taped it up, decorating the front of it with her own flair of cutout flowers and smiley faces drawn all over. When she handed it to me she gave me instructions not to open it until she went out. She said she knew I would probably cry and she didn't want to see that. She gave me a kiss, told me she loved me, wished me a Happy Mother's Day and went out for the evening. The note read:

Dear Mom,

Oprah suggested a few free, but priceless gifts to give for Mother's Day. This is mine to you.

I never realized how lucky I am to be alive until I realized how much you really love me. You have given me so much of your love and your time; you have made so many sacrifices for me and gone so far out of your way to help me and make sure I'm okay. I can't imagine how hard and stressful it was to raise two kids on your own, but you did it. I am proud of you for being able to manage Jack and I at the same time 24-7 for so many years. That alone is truly an accomplishment. I think about that picture of you and me when I was a sleeping little girl in your arms. That is a picture of unconditional love. I want to thank you. I thank you for keeping me; for giving me life. Thank you for raising me to be open-minded and unprejudiced, to choose my own religion, to say please and thank you, to be confident, to be strong, to stand up for myself, to be forgiving, to be generous, to fight with strong and effective words rather than my fists. These few words on a piece of paper can't say enough. But I hope they mean as much to you as I mean them to say. You are my best friend.

I really do appreciate you. I respect you. I love you!
Love Always, Your Daughter
She was right. I cried.

December 1993. DeAnne's disappearances became longer and longer periods of time, so when she turned eighteen it was no big deal when she moved in with a boyfriend. They chose to get an apartment in an area of South Minneapolis where most of the population was under thirty and chose to live in the old classic apartment buildings where rent was cheap. DeAnne bounced around the area doing temp jobs or waitressing but she always managed to take care of herself. The apartment they took was the upper level of a duplex. The stairs were rickety and the floor tiles were slightly wavy. But she was happy.

The first time she invited me over to her new apartment she fixed a delicious omelet while we sat in her kitchen and talked about her newfound independence. It suddenly felt like I was chatting with a friend. All of the hell that we went through together seemed to vanish. After we finished eating we went into her living room. She reached under the couch and pulled out a large wooden plate with at least a half ounce of weed scattered on it. It was the first time we smoked together even though we each knew the other one did. She opened a cabinet and took out a liter of vodka. Without even asking she poured me a shot, knowing I wouldn't refuse. She poured herself a glass of warm red wine and popped a Bob Marley tape into her boyfriend's massive stereo system. From that point on we always drank alcohol and smoked weed together. She admitted that there were other drugs she did occasionally, until I told her I didn't want to know. When her roomy walked in I tried not to react to his dirty, smelly appearance. Not dirty from just getting home from work – just plain stinky. He looked like a partying, don't-care kind of guy, which was where DeAnne was at. But the personal hygiene problem, I didn't get. ...but as long as he's nice to her, I thought.

Jack had been spending most of his time at his dad's house. When he got into junior high and high school he refused to wear his hearing aids and consequently failed everything. He too quit as soon as he turned sixteen. Up until he turned fifteen (in fact, I could swear it was on his fifteenth birthday), he was a great kid. Everyone he met liked him. He worried about me more than a child should have to, until suddenly he became someone else. He was mouthy and disrespectful toward me and constantly threatening physical violence toward DeAnne. His behavior became too much for me to handle so he was spending most of his time living with his dad, which also affected his choice to quit school, especially since transportation was an issue.

With neither of my kids living with me anymore I was forced to vacate the subsidized housing that I had lived and raised my children in for fifteen years. My feelings about my newfound independence were a mix of excitement and fear since I had never lived alone before. My apartment was cute and cozy. I loved it. It was close to the junior high where I worked as an assistant to special ed students. It seemed strange that after going through hell with both my kids in their adolescent years, I would choose to get a job working at a school with students who had behavior problems. It seemed to me that at least I had a lot of experience with troubled teens. My first assignment was to a student who had trashed a classroom and attempted to assault the teacher. He wasn't real happy to have a white female in her late thirties escorting him from class to class trying to help him maintain in the environment. He was black and twelve or thirteen when I started working with him. He hated me and everything and everyone else. No one thought he could or would be successful in the regular school programs so they started making arrangements for him to go to school elsewhere. But he did finish at that school. And he and I became very good friends. It was such a rewarding experience for me that I decided to continue working in the field.

February 1995. Shortly after moving into my own apartment I starting seeing the man I had met while attending a vocational school. It was just like old times. We spent much of our time drinking and dancing either at home or at a nightclub. We decided that after all that we had been through we still loved each other and thought we should get married. Neither of my kids, or anyone else, was fond of the idea. He was still as goofy and immature as always, but I liked him. With my lease almost up we decided to move into a house together while we made wedding plans. But it seemed that we were doomed almost from the day we moved in together.

I continued to work at the junior high, but he did nothing. Every day he had a new excuse as to why he wasn't looking for work. Several weeks into this behavior I told him I would not continue with wedding plans until he made some changes. One day he was supposed to pick me and a co-worker up after school and give us a ride home since my car was in the shop. Nearly an hour had passed before the other girl took another ride home while I continued to wait. When the building was about to close I called a cab and was livid when I got home and saw that his van was still in the garage, and I assumed he had fallen asleep. I unlocked the back door to a silent house and called out for him. No answer. Walking up the stairs to our bedroom I kept telling myself not to deck him. But he wasn't in the bedroom. I knocked on the bathroom door and heard nothing, so I opened it and found Norm passed out in the bathtub. There was an almost empty bottle of Captain Morgan's Rum sitting on the floor. The tub water was mixed with blood and vomit.

Grabbing the shower head while turning the faucet to cold I began spraying his face and body while screaming at him to wake up when suddenly I noticed the cuts across both of his wrists, the source of the blood in the bathwater. Running down the stairs to the phone the words I was screaming were not those of compassion, more of anger when I dialed 911. While talking with the operator I noticed a piece of paper on the table. It was a suicide letter. He decided that he wouldn't be able to find a job and that he knew I would leave him, something he could not handle. The police and EMT's arrived fairly quickly and dashed up the stairs. I could hear the pathetic sound of crying and felt no pity.

Soon after they took him away I called DeAnne and told her what had happened. Right away she told me to get out of my house and come to her apartment. I grabbed the 12-pack of beer I had in the refrigerator and left, unable to go back into the bathroom and clean up the mess. DeAnne and I sat for a few hours sharing stories about what losers men were while we smoked a little weed, had a few beers. When I felt that I could face what was waiting for me at home, she insisted on coming with me so I did not have to sleep alone in that house. As soon as we walked in the door she disappeared upstairs. When she returned she told me that she had cleaned the bathroom. The only thing she asked for in return was that I leave the guy once and for all.

December 27, 1995. DeAnne turned twenty-one. Hard to believe. She was always so mature for her age, but now she was a legal adult. Like most people her age on their twenty-first birthday, she wanted to go to a bar and drink – legally. Because she looked and acted so much older, and hung out with older people, she had been drinking in bars before. But now she could do it with her own I.D. She picked a bar in South Minneapolis where they played some great blues, inviting me and some of her friends to help her celebrate. We all got drunk and drove home.

We met at several bars after that for drinks. It was nice to have a friendly relationship with my daughter. She was on her own so I didn't have to worry about her sneaking out anymore. She never had to lie to me about what she did the night before because she was an adult now and I had no right to ask. Instead we became friends, very good friends. We talked on the phone several times a day. We shared stories about the guys we were dating. We rescued each other when times got tough. Many times she would send me little gifts in the mail with cutout flowers and smiley faces and a little note to cheer me up.

We were spending a lot of time drinking together, most times one or both of us would end up stumbling drunk. Sometimes we thought it was funny. Like the night we went to a neighborhood party. We had had way too much to drink and smoke and thought it was hilarious when DeAnne went to step up into the house and tipped straight backward instead, landing flat on her back. She felt no pain and was able to eventually make it safely into the house where she passed out on the couch. I went into the bathroom and puked. It wasn't funny.

Shortly after this incident my drinking had become a noticeable problem at work. Whether it was the morning breath, the mood swings, or the absenteeism to blame, my superiors suspended me until I went into treatment. It took a few days to build up the courage to seek out another program but my job was important to me so I checked into a program in Waverly. Between the effects of the withdrawal and my displeasure about being in another facility, no one was happy to see me, which was all right with me because I didn't really wanted to be bothered. The staff kept a close eye on me anyway because my blood pressure was so high and I was so sick. Within a week or so I started to mellow out a bit, but still maintained my distance from everyone. I just wanted my job back.

About halfway through my 28-day stay, my son's girlfriend gave birth to my first grandson. As soon as she went into labor I asked to be released long enough to be with her for the delivery, but it was not something they would allow. After a brief tantrum, I accepted their decision and waited until the wee hours of the morning to hear the news. As soon as I heard the phone ring at the nurse's desk I got up and ran down the hallway. "It's a boy!" my son proudly announced. My grandson was born eight weeks premature and had some serious but routine health problems expected with a premature baby, but I knew he was in good hands. After almost three months in the hospital, little Jack was allowed to go home.

Toward the end of my stay in Waverly, DeAnne decided to make a surprise visit to the treatment center. She borrowed a friend's truck, picked up my little Beagle, and began the one hour drive – drunk and without a driver's license. She never made it. Halfway through the trip DeAnne found herself sitting behind the wheel staring at a shattered windshield. She tried to open the driver's door but it was jammed. She pushed the door harder and with a loud creak it slowly opened just enough for her to get out. She walked around the front of the truck and noticed that the entire cab was crushed along with most of the front end. Someone approached her and told her that the police were on the way and that she should sit down. It took several minutes for her to realize that she had somehow lost control of the vehicle and rolled it into a ditch. The dog was still sitting in the front seat unharmed.

An ambulance was dispatched to the accident scene, but found the only thing wrong with DeAnne other than a few bumps and bruises was that she was drunk and did not have a license. She was then placed under arrest, while my dog was sent to the humane society until someone could pick her up. DeAnne faced several charges and as a result was sentenced to do time in the county workhouse. After that she was to check into an in-patient treatment program. The day she was released from the workhouse, her friend Keith picked her up on his motorcycle. She was so happy to be free and swore she would never be locked up again.

Somehow somewhere in between the workhouse and the treatment center DeAnne decided that she would rather not check into the facility. Instead she and Keith concocted a plan, unbeknownst to me, whereas Keith would drop her off with some friends who were on their way to Colorado. He was then planning to return to their apartment only to pick up their belongings then meet up with her out there and not return to Minnesota. At that point a warrant had been issued for DeAnne. Keith was not able to meet up with her as soon as he had planned however. Keith was flying down the freeway on his Harley when he lost control, sending both him and his bike catapulting down the road. He suffered road rash cuts across his face along with other serious injuries. He was taken to the hospital and treated for his injuries before he was arrested for driving while intoxicated. He was bailed out shortly after his arrest and came directly over to my apartment to let me know what had happened to both him and DeAnne. He apologized for contributing to her delinquency but claimed she begged him to help her get away so she wouldn't have to go into treatment. I really didn't know who I was angrier with at that point. Along with the legal consequences she now faced, she was farther away from me than she had ever been and that gave me a frightening and lonely feeling. She was always a phone call and only minutes away. Now I didn't know when I would be able to see or talk to her again. It made me nauseous to think about it.

We were able to talk on the phone quite often and she would still send me little notes with the cutout flowers and smiley faces. She would send me gifts that were covered in her "artwork." Just the packaging made me smile. She seemed to be quite happy in Colorado, but there were times that she would call drunk and crying. It was such a helpless feeling knowing that I couldn't just drive over to comfort her. Eventually, she and Keith broke up. Their relationship had been volatile at times, which worsened when they both drank. A short time after their break-up DeAnne hooked up with an old friend whom she had met when she lived in Minneapolis. They had always maintained a close, friendly relationship but had not become intimate until her relationship with Keith was supposedly over.

One night she called me in tears saying that her boyfriend, Mark, had gotten into some trouble and was going to have to go to jail for a long time. She was so afraid of being alone, but wouldn't consider coming back to Minnesota. She loved all of the places that she visited and lived in Colorado. She assured me she would be all right. She was always a most determined and capable person. It was just hard to hear her so sad so far away.

As soon as school ended for the year, so did my sobriety. It was almost planned. When I was forced into treatment by my employer in order to keep my job, I knew that I would only stay sober as long as I wanted and needed the job. But as soon as summer vacation came around it didn't matter what I did with my time. I had no one to account to and no one depending on me. My daughter was gone and my son was off spreading his wings with his buddies. There was no special man in my life, but still a few married men stopped by occasionally. The loneliness was beginning to get to me.

The worse I felt, the more I drank. The more I drank the worse I felt. I was in a downward spiral. Occasionally, I would get so drunk and depressed that I would get on the phone and talk desperately to anyone who would answer the phone, many times ending the conversation with the other person calling the police to check on me and make sure I didn't kill myself. When school started up again in the fall I applied at a different district. This way no one there would know of my history. My depression was deepening. Every day after punching out I wondered if I would be back the next day or if I would decide that suicide would be the better route before then.

The little house that I had been living in was in shambles. There were wasp nests between the walls in the front of the house and little red squirrels scurrying through the walls in the back. I had no hot water faucet in the kitchen and the bathroom had standing water so deep that I would sometimes wear plastic bags over my shoes to keep them from getting soaked. It was probably a good thing that the house was finally condemned but I was forced into making a move that I did not feel strong enough to do. A few weeks into my search a co-worker told me about a cute little house that was available for rent nearby. As soon as I looked at it I fell in love. It was nicer than any of the other places I had lived in.

During one of the school's summer breaks I took a job at a nearby hardware store. It was different than I was used to but it was interesting since I always did like tinkering with and trying to fix stuff myself. The store was located in a small shopping center along with a grocery and drug store and other novelty shops. Every morning the same UPS driver would stop by for our daily deliveries. He was easy to notice with his 6'4", 220 pound frame and body of solid muscle. He had grey hair and a thick mustache, with dimples that stretched the length of his masculine and chiseled cheeks. His hands were massive and strong like the rest of him.

We would exchange friendly banter every day and after a few months found that the conversations were becoming more personal. We met for lunch one afternoon in the mall where he admitted that he was married, but going through a divorce. We decided to meet that night and several nights after that. Three months into the relationship we realized that we were developing strong feelings toward each other. Almost two years later he moved into my little house. We had so many things in common to talk about and do together. We both loved being outdoors. Our first rendezvous was at a little place on the shore of Lake Superior where we spent many romantic moments near the water. Our biggest difference was the fact that I was an out of control alcoholic and he had been sober for more than 20 years. He told me several times how much he hated me drinking but then he would stop at the liquor store for me. Oftentimes however we would share a joint as soon as we finished our workday. In order to keep the peace I would sneak beers into the bathroom or the garage when he was sleeping or watching television so he wouldn't hear me pop the tops. Then I would quickly slam the beer and crunch the cans up as small as I could, then stash them near the bottom of the trash can.

September 9, 2001. This Sunday morning was much like many others. The little house had a fireplace in the living room so many nights we would haul the mattress out onto the living room floor where we could watch the fire in a more romantic setting. That is what we had decided to do that Saturday night. When we woke up the sun was barely peeking through the slits in between the blinds. We had left them lifted just enough to let a little of the fresh warm air in during the night. Before he woke up I grabbed a beer from the refrigerator and disappeared into the back bathroom. The water was already running when I coughed while secretly popping the top of the beer can. He was used to seeing me grab a cold one as soon as I woke up so when I returned to bed with the second beer he paid no attention. We packed a little weed in one of our pipes and took a couple of hits while we talked about our plans for the day. He stirred the coals up a little and added a few small logs before lying back down beside me on the mattress.

Unexpectedly we heard a car pull up in the driveway, just outside the open window. We heard car doors slam and footsteps approaching the front door. Suddenly we noticed what was clearly the uniform of a law enforcement officer showing through the small openings of the blinds. My boyfriend dashed into the bedroom while the officer began pounding on the door. Since I wasn't dressed I went to the kitchen window, which was too high for the officer to see directly into. I asked him if there was something I could help him with. He asked if my name was Mary. I told him it was.

He asked me to come to the door. Fearing that they found out I tested positive for marijuana use in a job application process the Friday before I told them I was not able to come to the door. He asked again if I would open the door. Once again I tried to put him off and asked if he could come back later. That didn't work either. He was determined to talk to me. I asked him if he would tell me what his visit was in regards to. He hesitated before asking me if I had a daughter named DeAnne. For a moment I felt relieved that the officer was not there to arrest me. It made sense that they would be asking about her since she still had an outstanding warrant. I answered him through the open window – yes, I have a daughter named DeAnne. There was another long pause before the officer continued, "Ma'am, I regret to inform you that your daughter was killed in an automobile accident last night."

Screaming hysterically, "NO, NO, NO!!!" I ran to the bedroom and blindly searched for a robe. My lover came from the bathroom, fastened up his jeans, and asked what was going on. The officers continued to pound on the door pleading with me to open it. "They said DeAnne is dead! It can't be right! Oh, God! NO, NO, NO!!!" Finally, we opened the door and let the officers in before I collapsed on the couch unable to catch my breath, my cries of terror and inconsolable grief filling the room. One of the officers tried to comfort me by placing his hand on my shoulder and telling me how sorry he was. The other officer went outside with my boyfriend. Several minutes later after asking and realizing that there was nothing they could do to help they apologized again for having to deliver the horrific news.

Denial was my only hope. There must have been some mistake. This can't be! This can't happen! She'll call. She'll call and tell me there was a terrible mistake. She's got to call! Please, please, DeAnne, I begged, please call me and tell me it was a mistake! She did not call. It was not a mistake. My baby, my beautiful baby girl was dead and there was nothing I could do about it.

For several minutes Dave and I lay together and cried. There was nothing he could say, nothing he could do to help. Finally I decided to call my sister, Danielle. She answered the phone sleepily and not too surprised to hear me crying on the other end. I told her she needed to go over to our mom's house right away. It seemed so wrong for me to say the words, so unreal, but somehow I had to say them. "DeAnne was killed last night. She was on the back of a speeding motorcycle when it crashed. She was killed instantly." The purging sobs that followed were inconsolable. "Please go to Mom's and tell her." (Since Dad had died from a number of health related issues a few years earlier, my mother was living alone.) As I was unable to make sense any more, Dave took the phone and told her what he knew from the officers, which wasn't much.

The next call was to my son who was in a long-term treatment program for help with his alcoholism. When Jack answered the phone all I could do was cry. How could I tell him that his sister had been killed? I couldn't. So I handed the phone to Dave. As soon as Jack heard the gruesome news the phone disconnected. Moments later it began to ring and when I picked it up all I could hear was sobbing. He begged me to tell him it wasn't true, but I couldn't. Before we hung up he said he would arrange a ride and get to my house as soon as he could.

A few hours later another police car pulled up in front of the house. The same officer that delivered the news was back. He apologized again for bothering me but informed me that the coroner in Colorado needed my phone number. The Coroner! Who is that? What is that for? I had no idea, except that it wasn't going to be good. It wasn't. Later that morning the phone rang and the person on the other end identified themselves as being from the Garfield County Coroner's Office. They apologized for my loss and went on to explain that they needed some information. First, they needed to identify the body. The body!? They were quite sure that the person in the morgue was my daughter but they wanted to know if she had any scars or tattoos to identify her. Somewhere around the time that DeAnne was "traveling" with her friends and trying new things, like coloring her hair green, she also decided to tattoo herself with that small peace sign on the back of her wrist. She was left-handed and the tattoo was on her right wrist. That was enough. The woman then went on to explain that since DeAnne's injuries were so severe an open casket would not be recommended. She said cremation was the best idea under the circumstances. WHAT! What was this person saying? Cremation! You mean burn my daughter! How dare she say these terrible things! I hung up without answering.

Several hours, phone calls, and beers later Danielle and Mom came over to console me and discuss what at that point made absolutely no sense to me, starting with the driver of the motorcycle. It was Keith. When Danielle told me it felt as if I had been punched in the stomach. I gagged and ran to the bathroom trying to vomit the nightmare. A few minutes later Dave came in and found me sitting on the floor of the bathroom sobbing. He helped me back onto my feet and into the living room where more misery was waiting. Keith and DeAnne were both drunk.

Shortly after they left a bar in Glenwood Springs, Colorado they got on Keith's bullet-bike. At a speed of over 100 m.p.h. he lost control of the bike and crashed into a concrete median. DeAnne flew off of the motorcycle and suffered many major injuries that killed her instantly. According to the officers, she probably had no idea what had happened. The officers arriving on the scene first found Keith staggering down the highway screaming and crying helplessly in the dark for DeAnne. It was that same officer who found DeAnne lying face down, her face against a boulder in the ditch. He knew immediately from the amount of blood and injuries to her that she was dead. Keith was taken by ambulance to the county hospital where his injuries were found to be non life threatening. While he was still in the emergency room, two police officers came in and placed him under arrest for vehicular homicide. All Keith wanted to do at that point was trade his life for hers.

DeAnne's boyfriend at the time had been about halfway through his sentence of 90 days in the county workhouse. That night he was out on a pass but was expected to return by midnight. His plan was to spend some time alone with his girlfriend before checking in. He waited impatiently, knowing she was with Keith. By 11:15 he had to give up waiting so he could catch the last bus back into town. As the bus drove down the same highway where the accident had just occurred Mark wondered where DeAnne was that she wasn't able to meet him. He checked back into the jail just before midnight and returned to his cell hurt and confused. Around 2 a.m. one of the guards went into Mark's cell. He gave him a nudge to wake him and ordered him to get up and follow him into another area where a chaplain was waiting. He knew in his heart something terrible had happened but he was not prepared to hear that DeAnne was dead.

During that time we were all in a state of shock, disbelief, wanting to trade our lives for hers. Keith, Mark, and me. But I had to stay as sane and sober as I could in order to do the things I had to do, things I didn't understand, things I had never been prepared to handle. My sister was able to contact the necessary people regarding DeAnne's remains and her memorial service.

When the time came for me to make the decision to have DeAnne cremated it felt as if my life would end with hers. No matter how much I wanted to block the images of her beautiful smile, her long blonde hair, her incredible dimples and green eyes going through the cremation process, I could not escape them. Every waking moment I was haunted by the visions of her flying that 250 feet before she hit the pavement. Or the sight that officer must have seen that made him know immediately that she was dead.

September 11, 2001. Danielle scheduled an appointment for us to meet with someone from the Cremation Society at 10 a.m. My son and his girlfriend were planning to pick me up a little before nine to meet my sister and mother there. As soon as my son walked in the door he asked if I heard what happened in New York as he turned the television on. At that very moment the second plane hit. For a moment I did not feel so alone. Suddenly there were so many people who were about to suffer the same grief I was experiencing.

My sister and mother were already in the parking lot waiting for us when we arrived. I did not want to get out of the car. As I walked across the parking lot, I felt as if my legs were heavy and weak. Regardless of my pleas not to make me go into the building my family reminded me that I had no choice. Shortly after we entered the building a man in his late 40's wearing the customary black suit and tie came in and welcomed us. He expressed his routine condolences and led us downstairs to a conference room with a large table and several chairs.

We sat in that room for nearly two hours planning DeAnne's memorial like we were planning a birthday party for her. What did I want the announcement to include? Where did I want the memorial to take place? What about the music? Did I want a priest to orate? Who did I want to talk about her? What about an urn? That was the one that really hurt. The man opened a photo album that he had had sitting in front of him. He began to sell his products as if I was ordering her birthday cake. When I told him I didn't know what to do and that I didn't have any money he told me that if I did not buy an urn my daughter would be coming home in a plastic bag. He modeled the bag by putting his hands in the shape of a small loaf of bread as he spoke the words. I told him I would have to let him know. Before we left the meeting, he handed me a bill for $1400.

For the next few days I did not want to talk to anyone or do anything but drink and sleep. There were many times however that I was forced to deal with things I did not want to deal with. It was just too horrific. But everyone needed some answers to what I wanted to do.

Mark was released early from his sentence because of the circumstances and his good behavior while in jail. His parents immediately flew to Colorado to help and support him however they could. Fortunately he and his parents were able to take care of the necessities in Colorado, including finding a beautiful Aspen box, so she did not have to come home in a plastic bag.

Because of the terrorist attacks on New York all air traffic had come to a halt. Consequently Mark and his parents were stranded in Colorado. They made several attempts to fly home but their efforts were futile, so they extended their car rental agreement and drove back to Minnesota. As soon as they arrived home they called to let me know that I could pick up my daughter. Throughout the long ride to their home the pit of my stomach ached, my heart hurt, and my head felt like it was going to explode. By the time we arrived I could not breathe and did not want to move. Mark saw us pull up and came out to the car. We held each other and shared helpless sobs as he escorted me into the house. My knees were shaking so badly that I could not stand on my own. He led me to a chair in the living room where his parents were waiting. They apologized for my loss. I thanked them for bringing her home. Mark disappeared for a moment while I waited for him to come out and tell me it was a mistake and bring DeAnne out from the other room. Instead he came out with a dark blue felt satchel about the size of a small pillow case. He walked over and set the case in my lap. No one spoke. No one knew what to say. Mark loosened the gold tie around the top of the satchel and opened it just enough to show me the light colored box with a beautiful green stone in the corner, a color near the color of my baby's eyes. There was nothing anyone could say so Mark and Dave walked us back out to the car.

September 16, 2001. It wasn't until we reached the chapel at the Cremation Society that I opened the satchel. Inside the chapel was a small white pedestal waiting for us. While Dave held the satchel I slowly and carefully lifted the beautiful box from it and placed her remains on the pedestal. I fell into a nearby chair as more reality began to sink in and I became weak with grief. Soon after, family members started to arrive. An hour later more and more people began to gather in the chapel, each of them offering hugs and condolences. I just wanted to take my daughter and leave.

One of my sisters had agreed to find appropriate music for the service. She began with the traditional Amazing Grace. Halfway through the service a strong yet beautiful voice filled the air with the song "Somewhere Over the Rainbow." I wanted to hear my daughter's angelic voice sing it to me. But I knew I would never hear her sing it again. It was almost too much for me to bear.

Shortly after the introductory music ended the priest entered the room. He began his prayers and readings from the Bible. Inviting the priest was not what I had chosen for myself, since Catholicism was no longer something I followed. But for my mother's sake it only seemed appropriate to invite him. He spoke for several minutes, not once making mention of DeAnne's mother. He was just there to do his job. However, at the end of the service he overstepped his bounds a little by telling me I was supposed to put her remains in the ground as the Bible intended. My initial reaction was, who did he think he was to be telling me what I should do with my daughter! With insincere respect I told the priest I intended to take my baby home.

The service was over in about thirty minutes. It seemed like hours. The two hundred or so people who attended extended their condolences again before the chapel emptied. DeAnne's stepfather, Todd, was also in attendance. Just as we were about to leave he came over to me and asked if he could carry her out to the car. For a moment I was able to forgive him for all of his sick and evil past behavior. He took the box that had been rewrapped in the dark blue bag and said tearfully, "This is about how big she was when I carried her out of the hospital."

Dave and I took my daughter's remains home and decided we needed to get away for a short time, just to catch our breath. We placed the box on the living room table, then put a few things in an overnight bag and left. It didn't feel right leaving her sitting on the table by herself, but I needed to get away. We headed toward Duluth, a place where we knew we would find peace and fresh air. It was the off season for tourists so not everything was open, but we managed to find a little ma-'n-pa resort with little rickety, worn down cabins. Just perfect, we thought. The air was a little too chilly next to the lake to have the windows open, but we were desperate for some fresh air. We opened the windows and put a few extra blankets on the bed. Before retiring we knew we needed a walk, so we wandered down toward the rocky shore of Lake Superior, the waves crashing against the huge rocks that were scattered along the beach. Neither of us felt like talking as we strolled hand-in-hand along the shore. We both knew that we had to go back and face more ugliness, but for the moment it was so peaceful.

Mid-October 2001. It was understandable that anyone suffering this kind of loss would no doubt need some professional help. I called a therapist I had visited in the past and began seeing her on a weekly basis. Regardless of her help I continued to drink and eat only sleeping pills, narrowly missing an overdose of the combination many times. My relationship with Dave was crashing because of it. He felt helpless and exhausted. One morning when I had left for an appointment with my counselor he decided he could not take it anymore. He could not stand watching me destroy myself, and he recognized I was taking him down with me. I came directly home from my appointment, having been gone no more than a couple of hours. When I walked in the door I knew immediately that something wasn't right. I glanced over at the dining room table and noticed a sticky note attached to the table. It said, "Sorry it had to be like this. Don't call me." I ran to the closets and the garage and found every trace of him gone. Before I shed a tear I got back in the car and drove straight to the liquor store.

My son called shortly after I returned with the case of beer. As soon as I told him what had happened he hung up the phone, checked out of his treatment program, and showed up at my door within a few hours. He was terrified that I would kill myself. He knew that I had seriously contemplated suicide many times throughout my life, so he was correct in assuming this might just be the thing to push me over the edge.

Jack had been in a few treatment programs prior to the one he was in at that time. He never really seemed interested in changing his lifestyle. It's just that he needed three hots and a cot when any girl he'd been dating would throw him out. He had never had his own place, a car, or even a job for more than two weeks because he chose to have his life revolve around alcohol. It only took him a matter of a few hours to join me in a beer. Since I didn't want him giving me a hard time about my drinking I felt I couldn't condemn him for his so we drank together day after day after day.

Two weeks after Jack and I began our binge my body started rejecting my behavior. It was common behavior for me to vomit on a daily basis, even though there was nothing in my stomach except the burning, sour taste of bile. One morning during my vomiting routine I noticed blood in the toilet. Eventually there was more and more. Since I had had this problem several years before I knew I was in trouble. Part of me kept thinking I should just keep doing what I was doing so I could be with my daughter. But my son became very concerned. He talked to one of my sisters on the phone, telling her about my health. The next time I talked to her I got an earful. The end result was that she and Jack decided that if I didn't agree to go into some kind of in-patient treatment immediately they would call 911 and have me hospitalized. Not really having an alternative, except to go ahead and kill myself, I agreed to check into another program.

November 1, 2001. My sister picked me up early to meet the 10 a.m. appointment we had scheduled for me to check into the treatment facility. It was all too familiar to me right from the moment we walked into the reception area. The paperwork was all the same. The questions were all the same. The admissions people were all the same. Many times I considered running out the door and down the street away from this experience, but I was feeling so physically lousy I knew I wouldn't have made it very far.

When I finished completing all of the paperwork we were given another address a few miles away where the women's program was located. The building itself was different than the others I had been in. This was a large house, one that had been previously used as a model home. There was another house on the same lot where the staff lived and meetings were held. The client's house was clean and modern, and busy and loud. The house seemed big from the outside, but after checking in and being told I was sharing it with 20 other women, the house became very, very small. My sister left as soon as she could, fearing I might talk her into taking me home. The thought definitely crossed my mind, especially when I was led downstairs into a room just large enough for five single beds and five small dressers. The only place to sit was on the bed – and I would never be alone. Privacy was out of the question. But when I arrived all of the other women were in groups. I put my clothes in the tiny dresser and unpacked a small box that my sister had given me before leaving. Inside was a delicate and beautiful crystal angel. As soon as I placed the angel in the window the walls and bed were covered with tiny little rainbow images. I tried to count how many but there too many to count. Suddenly I felt as if DeAnne had wrapped her comforting arms around me.

The next several days were very trying for me, the other women, and the staff because of my bitterness about being there. No one, including the staff, could possibly understand what I was going through at the time. Not only had I just lost my daughter in a tragic accident, but my boyfriend moved out on me soon after, and now my dear friend 'alcohol' wasn't there for me either. My fits of anger had become almost intolerable for the staff. I was snapping at everyone and at one point when I was told I could not use the phone I came very close to ripping it out of the wall. After that outburst, the counselors suggested that I might be better off in a psychiatric facility. To me, that was not an option, so I tried to be a little more cooperative.

A week or so into the program I finally opened up to the group about what happened to DeAnne. Until that time no one really knew what was going on with me. When the group ended the other clients opened their arms to me and forgave me for my state of mind up to that point. When I was physically able I asked the staff if I could leave the grounds to run. They not only approved, they encouraged me. Every day starting a few days after I arrived and every day after I would put on the walkman my sister had given me as incentive and run two miles. By the time I left I had regained several of the thirty-some pounds I had lost and felt better than I had in a very long time.

Most of the reading and writing segments of the program were routine for me. Except for one. One of the counselor's had given me an assignment to read a booklet on the consequences of alcohol. After reading it I was required to write a report on what I got out of it. It was during this assignment that I realized the most serious consequence as a result of my alcoholic behavior. It was losing my daughter in a drunken driving accident.

Suddenly I realized that my behavior may have been instrumental in my daughter's death. Throughout most of her life she only knew me drunk. She saw me get behind the wheel after drinking. She would see me with one beer in my purse and another in the glove compartment. She rode right next to me many times when I drove to the liquor store, already drunk. When she became of legal age to drink in bars we would go out and drink together and I would drive us home. Why should she think it was wrong or dangerous to get in or on a vehicle with someone who'd been drinking when I did it with her all the time?

The responsibility that I felt in her death became my strength. DeAnne always wanted me to quit drinking. She knew all too well how alcohol would change my personality and cause my depression to spiral. As she got older she realized the effect that it also had on my health. She wanted me sober. So, for her, I knew I needed to change. Many counselors would tell me that I need to stay sober for me, but that didn't work. Even now, if I were to choose what I felt was best for me, I would drink myself to death. Through all of the programs I participated in I wish that someone had told me to stop thinking about myself and think about what I was doing to my children.

April 2002. The sentencing part of Keith's trial came eight months after the accident. Until that point he had not served one day in jail. When I first heard of the accident, that he was the driver, I felt more forgiveness than anger. How could I be angry with him when I drove drunk with her so many times in the past? It could just as well have been me driving her. Besides, how could I blame him when I felt as if I had handed her the keys and given her permission to get on that bike? What bothered me the most was the fact that Keith never accepted responsibility, outside of his initial reaction immediately after the accident. After that he pleaded "not guilty" and was allowed to go home with his parents. I didn't think I had the energy to battle him or the legal system so I didn't. But when I got a letter saying there was a chance he would only be sentenced to probation I became irate with both him and the system. So when I asked to attend the sentencing hearing by a representative of the Colorado Victim's Unit, I made arrangements and flew down there.

November 2002. Several months after becoming sober, Dave and I began seeing each other again. When he saw how much more healthy and peaceful I was he decided to move back in with me. He expressed his pride many times over, while at the same time fearing the day he would come home from work and find me drunk. With the help of a women's AA group that I attended weekly, the love and support of my family, son, and Dave, I was able to get through some very difficult times the first few years. The women in the group frequently expressed their admiration for my emotional strength. Yet it was impossible for me to accept the compliment when I felt so weak and damaged inside.

Fall 2003. It didn't take long to discover that my little house just wasn't big enough for Dave and me. Since we both liked Northern Minnesota so much we decided to look for something in Brainerd. We found a beautiful new lake home that was available during the off-season months of September through May. But the transition was difficult. Between his problems controlling his anger and my emotional instability we questioned our relationship and our decision to move many times, but we always managed to work through the rough spots.

A few months after moving I felt the need to get some counseling again. I called one of only a few listings for mental health offices in the area and was introduced to a woman about my age that made me feel comfortable as soon as we started talking. We began meeting once a week, an appointment I looked forward to since I didn't know anyone else in the area. She was always so attentive, soft-spoken, and wise. Just her presence was calming. Her true compassion and appropriate suggestions helped me gradually get stronger with each session.

December 2004. After our lease had expired we moved into a cute little place with a lot of acreage full of farmland and forestry. It was so peaceful. My son was still battling his demons. His alcoholic behavior had gotten him in trouble again. If he wasn't slapping around his girlfriend physically and emotionally, he had the law after him. He went to jail a couple of times for alcohol-related offenses and at this point was required, as part of his probation, to check into another in-patient treatment program. Since he had no place to live at the time we allowed him to stay with us through the holidays so he could spend time with his son.

His probation officer was able to locate a facility near my home where Jack could have support from me. It was a great relief to both of us when he found one just ten miles away. While he was there we visited when we could, but talked every day, sometimes several times a day. He seemed to be sincere about wanting to turn his life around, so I gladly attended his family group sessions and did whatever else I could to show him my support.

The program was to have lasted 60 days. He made it about twenty. He was so distracted with his hormones that he refused to think about anyone or anything else. It wasn't until he left (or was asked to leave) that one of his counselors told me that he was not respectful of the program or anyone in it. She said they had given him several chances and breaks because they liked the kid. But he was manipulating all of us. The day he left the program he called – and wished he hadn't. I was furious. And hurt. He betrayed me with his lies and conning ways. How could he do this to me? More importantly, how could he do this to his sister? At that point I decided I had to remove myself from him and his destructive behavior. There had been so many times when I was there for him when he was in need of help with his alcoholism because, as with DeAnne, I felt some responsibility. But it had reached the point where was I feeling used. I had to make the decision to let someone else help him. It was not an easy choice to refuse a relationship with him, but I knew it was what I had to do.

March 2004. Just before Jack left his program a local television station called. Through a friend the reporter heard about my story. He asked if he could do a story about DeAnne and me. The friend told him how I felt partly responsible for my daughter's death. He believed that sharing my experience and my feelings with other people may help to save someone else's life. The reporter agreed to come to our house with a photographer. They both were very friendly, making me feel relaxed in front of the camera. We sat across from each other and talked for almost an hour. He asked a question occasionally, but most of the time I talked about how my daughter's death was a painful wake-up call.

Around this same time I had called Jack's former counselor from the treatment center. She agreed to meet with me and discuss what had happened while he was there. It was almost embarrassing. But during the conversation she and I began discussing the possibility of my being a guest speaker at their family group meetings. Since many people kept telling me I had something important to share I decided to keep talking and agreed to speak once a month. Each time was draining, reliving those terrible thoughts and images over and over. But each time at the end of the meetings when the clients would come up to me offering hugs and thanks, I left feeling stronger than when I went in. It was obvious that sharing my experience was making a difference, so I kept on talking. The more I spoke at various impact panels, treatment facilities, and other safe and sober programs the more I learned about myself and the stronger I became.

Since I began my journey with sobriety I have learned many valuable things. They have helped me during those times when staying sober has been a struggle. Some are the very things I rebelled against in the treatment programs and AA meetings I attended, and they have now become my greatest sources of strength. The words of the Serenity Prayer for example were hard for me to grasp. Since it is usually the opening or closing prayer of alcoholic gatherings, be it in a treatment facility or an AA meeting, I was constantly reciting the words. But because I wasn't a real religious person, getting past the first word, God, was difficult. At some point I found myself saying, Mary, grant yourself some peace of mind and accept the things you cannot change. Be courageous enough to change what you can. And be wise enough to know the difference. By reciting these words I have been able to do things, and survive things, that I never thought I could or would.

Accepting that there is nothing I can do to bring my daughter back is the hardest truth to face. After recovering from the initial insanity that followed the announcement of her death I have had to accept that her love and her spirit are all that I have left. I long to hear her voice and touch her beautiful face but I cannot change the painful reality that that will never be. Instead I am left with the uncontrollable visions of my baby flying through the air, hitting the ground, landing in a ditch, bleeding to death, then going through the cremation process.

I have had to accept that there will always be questions that I may never have the answers to:

Was she laughing at the time or screaming at him to slow down? Why did she lay in the ditch for three and a half hours before they moved her body? Has Keith changed his lifestyle as a result of this deadly choice? Would seeing him or talking with him make any real difference to me?

One of the questions that has and always will haunt me is: If I had raised DeAnne to understand that she should never get in or on a vehicle with someone who had been drinking, could I have saved her life that night? Having to accept this unanswered question is the most difficult.

Grief and sadness are a permanent part of my life. Losing my daughter was the worst thing that will ever happen to me, I know that for sure. At times that is my consolation, along with the fact that my daughter knew how much I loved her when she died. I cry a lot and have days when the inescapable heartache paralyzes me. That pain will never go away.

Finding the courage to stay sober is a constant challenge, but with the love and support of the people who care about me, as well as my commitment to DeAnne, I have been able to maintain my sobriety. On the day of my fifth anniversary I better understood why counselors kept telling me that I needed to find sobriety for myself. Since I loved my kids as much as I did I felt they should have been my motivation to stay sober, but I kept hearing, "You need to do this for yourself." My alcoholic behavior was so selfish, it seemed silly not to be encouraged do it for my children. But on this day I discovered why it is so important to stay sober for myself.

It was a big day for me. I had hoped that my supporters would recognize the day and find reason to celebrate with me. But no one remembered. It was a very lonely place to be, but it was where I needed to be to better understand why it is also so important to stay sober for myself. Although a pat on the back, or one of the anniversary medallions, would have been nice, I suddenly felt real pride in myself, for myself.

Part of my healing has also been in finding the courage to change the things I can. First and most importantly I have to find the courage to stay sober. It is very difficult, especially when I feel under a great deal of stress or depression. During those times when I feel the strongest desire to drink, I see myself putting a loaded gun in my mouth – not just a drink. I cannot do that to DeAnne.

Having the ability to stand in front of a group of people and accept responsibility for my mistakes as a parent while sharing my experience with other people has surprised many people, including myself. Most of my life I have been in the shadows, sometimes by choice because I was so insecure. I could never have imagined myself being able to talk in front of a small group of people, much less a large one. But I have, hoping maybe the life of another mother's daughter, or anyone else, might be saved.

There are moments when I get confused about the things I can and cannot change. But through the guidance of many and the spirit of DeAnne I always seem to be able to figure it out. Accepting that I cannot change the past has been very difficult, but anyone who reads this has the ability to change the future, with courage and wisdom. Peace.

For more than twenty years I had
kept a disorganized journal.
It is with those notes and recent events
that I have written this story.
Out of respect for the other people included in this book
all of the names have been changed
with the exception of mine and DeAnne's.

It is through the help of the following people
that I am able to share this story
with the hope that it will save another mother's daughter:

Kathleen Marusak, Editor (kathleen_editor@yahoo.com)
Tammy Wippler, Cover Design (tlwippler@charter.net)
Patty Jo and Noreen, Therapists and Friends
Debbie, My Sister and Mentor
A Special Thanks to My Best Friend, Donny,
Who has been my constant source of encouragement.

Thank-You to All of You!

www.ingramcontent.com/pod-product-compliance
Lightning Source LLC
Chambersburg PA
CBHW072133280526
45788CB00002B/623